Yale Studies in English

Benjamin Christie Nangle, Editor

VOLUME 145

Published with aid from the

foundation established in memory of

Philip Hamilton McMillan

of the class of 1894, Yale College

E. D. HIRSCH, JR.

Wordsworth and Schelling

A TYPOLOGICAL STUDY

OF ROMANTICISM

NEW HAVEN: YALE UNIVERSITY PRESS, 1960

© 1960 by Yale University Press, Inc.
Set in Baskerville type
and printed in the United States of America by
Vail-Ballou Press, Inc., Binghamton, New York
and reprinted by The Carl Purington Rollins Printing-Office
of the Yale University Press, New Haven, Connecticut.

First published, March, 1960
Second printing, November, 1960

47,765,
August, 1964

To my mother and father

The Philip Hamilton McMillan Memorial

Publication Fund

The present volume is the fifty-ninth work published by the Yale University Press on the Philip Hamilton McMillan Memorial Publication Fund. This foundation was established December 12, 1922, by a gift to Yale University in pursuance of a pledge announced on Alumni University Day in February, 1922, of a fund of $100,000 bequeathed to James Thayer Mc-Millan and Alexis Caswell Angell, as Trustees, by Mrs. Elizabeth Anderson McMillan, of Detroit, to be devoted by them to the establishment of a memorial in honor of her husband.

He was born in Detroit, Michigan, December 28, 1872, prepared for college at Phillips Academy, Andover, and was graduated from Yale in the Class of 1894. As an undergraduate he was a leader in many of the college activities of his day, and within a brief period of his graduation was called upon to assume heavy responsibilities in the management and direction of numerous business enterprises in Detroit, where he was also Trustee of the Young Men's Christian Association and of Grace Hospital. His untimely death, from heart disease, on October 4, 1919, deprived his city of one of its leading citizens and his University of one of its most loyal sons.

Preface

I HAVE TAKEN Wordsworth quotations from *The Poetical Works of William Wordsworth,* ed. Ernest de Selincourt and Helen Darbishire, 5 vols. London, Oxford University Press, 1940–49. Quotations from *The Prelude* are in every case from the early (1805–06) version in *The Prelude or Growth of a Poet's Mind,* ed. Ernest de Selincourt, London, Oxford University Press, 1926. In quoting fragments, variant readings, or poetry not published elsewhere, I supply page references to *The Poetical Works* (sometimes, for the sake of clarity, referred to in the notes as Wordsworth). In other cases I simply give the title of the poem and the line numbers. Schelling is quoted from *Schellings Sämtliche Werke,* ed. K. F. A. Schelling, 14 vols. Stuttgart, 1856–61. This edition appears in two divisions. The first ten volumes (Part I) contain works published by Schelling. The second four (Part II) contain the posthumous works. I shall designate the volume numbers as a series, from one through fourteen. Thus, volume 3 in Part I will appear as 3, volume 2 in Part II as 12. This method is simpler and immediately provides the reader with a hint as to chronology since the edition is ordered chronologically. I do not reproduce Schelling's frequent double spacing of words because he is often emphasizing a point in his argument which is quite different from the point that is important for my purposes. The emphases have little meaning in isolated quotations and they tend to be misleading. Translations are mine unless otherwise credited. Where a translation appears in the text I have given merely the reference at the bottom of the page, in order not to encumber the page; the original German (sometimes fuller than the passage translated) is given in the appendix.

In its present form (except for revision in the Introduction and the last chapter) this study was presented as a doctoral dissertation at Yale University. It is the direct result of the stimulation I received in two graduate seminars at Yale, one on the Romantic Age, conducted by F. A. Pottle, and the other on the philosophy of Hegel, conducted by G. A. Schrader. To Professor Pottle, my adviser, I owe a special debt of gratitude for the much-needed encouragement he supplied in the early days of the undertaking when I was foundering upon "strange seas of thought alone." After my return from a year's study in Germany, made possible by a Fulbright grant, Professor Pottle criticized each newly written chapter promptly and in detail. Although I have specifically acknowledged (in Chapter 7) only one of his suggestions, I have taken advantage of many others. Numerous conversations with my friend, Klaus Hartmann, of Bonn University, illuminated German philosophy for me. Cleanth Brooks, Charles Feidelson, Maynard Mack, Martin Price, and George Schrader were all kind enough to read through the manuscript and make suggestions for its improvement. I am obliged to Diana T. Waugh for her many hours of detailed work in helping get the manuscript in final shape for the printer.

I am grateful to the Fund for Young Scholars for assistance in publication of the book. Displeasing as it may be to her, I also render public thanks to my wife for her encouragement and assistance in the job of revising the Introduction and final chapter.

E. D. H., Jr.

New Haven,
September 15, 1959

Contents

1. Introduction

THERE IS SOME VIRTUE in the simplified sort of literary history which marks the beginning of romanticism in England by the epochal date 1798, the year when Wordsworth and Coleridge published *Lyrical Ballads*. For although everything in *Lyrical Ballads* had its roots in established conventions and attitudes, although no detail lacked precedent, the gross anatomy of the whole was new and strange. The poetry's idiom, especially the idiom of "Tintern Abbey," was different in kind from that of any previous English poetry. In his "Advertisement" to *Lyrical Ballads*, Wordsworth, who wrote all but four of the twenty-three poems, frankly or apologetically asked that they "be considered as experiments," and he accurately predicted that readers would "frequently have to struggle with feelings of strangeness and aukwardness." Of course, *Lyrical Ballads* cannot be designated the source of romanticism in England, but it can be viewed as its first fully articulate expression.

A few months before the appearance of *Lyrical Ballads*, Schelling came forward in Leipzig with the first of his books in *Naturphilosophie*. Written and published in 1797, the *Ideen zu einer Philosophie der Natur* showed clearly that he was an independent thinker and not merely

1

a disciple of Fichte. In earlier works (*Vom Ich als Prinzip der Philosophie*, 1795; *Abhandlungen zur Erläuterung des Idealismus der Wissenschaftslehre*, 1796–97) Schelling still ambiguously adhered to the notion in Fichte's *Wissenschaftslehre* of a free, all encompassing, yet fundamentally human ego. But in the *Ideen* Schelling comes into his own; Fichte's view is sensed as being one-sided; explicitly poised against the "Ich" is an equally real and equally important "Natur." Especially in the introduction to the *Ideen* it is apparent that Schelling has broken through the subjective barrier. Man and Nature, Thought and Being, Subject and Object, I and Not-I must always be taken together as interdependent poles of a single cosmic reality. This is the new voice of German romantic philosophy.

The chronological closeness of *Lyrical Ballads* and the *Ideen* symbolizes an astonishing spiritual closeness between Wordsworth and Schelling. The near congruence of the two dates, 1797 and 1798, may not, perhaps, prove the existence of a homogeneous *Zeitgeist*, but the similarity between the two writers does lend force to the view that romanticism is a meaningful historical term, a view which Wellek has defended against Lovejoy's discrimination of romanticisms.[1] No doubt Lovejoy is right to insist that not everyone who has been called a romantic ought to be so called, but I do think it makes sense to think of romanticism as a unitary and international movement. Not everyone, of course, in the late eighteenth and early nineteenth century belonged to the movement, but those who actually did may be identified not by the fact that they displayed an array of isolated characteristics but by the fact that they shared a certain type of Weltanschauung. To the extent that this was in fact the case, "romanticism"

1. A. O. Lovejoy, "On the Discrimination of Romanticisms," *PMLA*, *39* (1924), 229–53. René Wellek, "The Concept of 'Romanticism' in Literary History," *Comparative Literature*, *1* (1949), 1–23, 147–72.

has a definite and unitary meaning. And I do not see how the similarities between Wordsworth and Schelling can be explained except on the hypothesis that both shared the same type of Weltanschauung.

The similarities cannot be explained convincingly by positing an influence of Schelling on Wordsworth. As to direct influence, Wordsworth knew too little German to be affected directly by anything written in that language, and in later life he was content to announce that he had "never read a word of German metaphysics, thank Heaven." [2] By an indirect path, however, some notion of German philosophy must have come to him by 1844, when he pronounced: "Kant, Schelling, Fichte; Fichte, Schelling, Kant: all this is dreary work and does not denote progress." [3] But these later comments indicate nothing about the young Wordsworth. In the period of the Great Decade (1797–1806) not even Coleridge knew Schelling. In spite of that "genial coincidence" between the views of the two men, Coleridge makes no mention of Schelling in letters or criticism through 1806. In the newly published *Notebooks* (1794–1804) there is no reference to Schelling, and Miss Coburn, the editor, states bluntly that by "Sept 1800, Coleridge had not read Schelling." [4] Before 1801 Coleridge, according to Wellek, had no significant knowledge even of Kant.[5] And in 1798, with *Lyrical Ballads* behind them, when Coleridge and the Wordsworths went to Germany, few of Schelling's own countrymen had heard of him.

2. *Correspondence of Crabb Robinson with the Wordsworth Circle*, ed. Edith Morley (2 vols. Oxford, Clarendon Press, 1927), *1*, 401.

3. *Memories of Old Friends, being Extracts from the Journals and Letters of Caroline Fox*, ed. H. N. Pym (2d ed. Philadelphia, 1884), p. 215; cited by M. L. Peacock, Jr., in *The Critical Opinions of William Wordsworth*, Baltimore, Johns Hopkins Press, 1950.

4. *The Notebooks of Samuel Taylor Coleridge*, ed. Kathleen Coburn (New York, Pantheon, 1957), *1* (notes), n. to entry 787.

5. René Wellek, *Immanuel Kant in England, 1793–1838* (Princeton, Princeton Univ. Press, 1931), p. 72.

All this makes it seem unlikely that Schelling influenced Wordsworth in the Great Decade, the period with which this study deals. But one further circumstance makes the question of influence seem almost irrelevant. Some of Schelling's root ideas first make their appearance in 1797, in the introduction to the *Ideen*. On the other hand, all of Wordsworth's root ideas, all the many notions common to Wordsworth and Schelling, are implicit in "Tintern Abbey," composed in July of 1798. It seems reasonable, then, to assume that Schelling's philosophy in no way influenced Wordsworth's fundamental attitudes and ideas.

To explain the similarities of the two writers we are thrown back to the simple hypothesis that Wordsworth and Schelling developed independently an identical Weltanschauung. The hypothesis is not implausible. In the 1790's England and Germany were not isolated cultures but were open to currents vibrating all of Western Europe. Both men inherited, for example, the assumption that nature is perspicuously ordered; both sympathized strongly with the French revolutionaries and their ideals; both, it may be added, grew up in the country and formed an early love for the natural landscape.

Thousands, of course, must have undergone similar influences without developing a similar view of the world; in the 1790's, as in any other period, one man's meat is another's poison. A central fact about human selfhood is its diversity. But selfhood is organic; its components tend to sustain one another in a dynamic unity which remains self-identical through the temporal stream of experience. Now, if a Weltanschauung is understood as a type of cultural selfhood, then it is not difficult to conceive how Wordsworth and Schelling developed an identical Weltanschauung.[6] If it happened, for example, that they both

6. Cultural subjectivity, as opposed to private, incommunicable mental processes has been brilliantly defined by Eduard Spranger, "Zur Theorie

firmly sensed the divinity of nature, this belief, along with its inherited assumptions, would have implied other beliefs, feelings, attitudes, ideas, and patterns of thought. In such a process of mutual implication outside influences are not always decisive. A Weltanschauung is not a mere nexus of causes; it is an organic system, a cultural selfhood with a logic and autonomy of its own. This, I think, is the most probable "explanation" of the remarkable congruence between Wordsworth and Schelling.

I am not, of course, the first to notice the congruence. Years ago, A. C. Bradley said bluntly that Wordsworth's poetry and German philosophy expressed "the same mind," and less Hegelian critics like J. W. Beach have suggested hesitantly that the Germans might have influenced Wordsworth.[7] Bradley's view is, I think, the truer one, and also holds out the prospect of an interesting inquiry. Why did Englishmen and Germans independently develop notions like the remarkable one that everything, including rocks and stones, is alive? For a modern mind, one of the fascinations of German romantic philosophy is its apparent extravagance. A poet is supposed to be imaginative; often his expressions are supposed to be taken in a Pickwickian sense. But how could any finely organized intellect entertain seemingly ridiculous notions as ultimate, philosophic truth? The question cannot be answered simply by referring to intellectual, political, and economic

---

des Verstehens und zur geisteswissenschaftlichen Psychologie" in *Festschrift Johannes Volkelt zum 70. Geburtstag,* Munich, 1918. See esp. p. 369.

7. A. C. Bradley, *Oxford Lectures on Poetry* (2d ed. London, Macmillan, 1909), p. 129: "His poetry is immensely interesting as an imaginative expression of the same mind which, in his day, produced in Germany great philosophies. His poetic experience, his intuitions, his single thoughts, even his large views, correspond in a striking way, sometimes in a startling way, with ideas methodically developed by Kant, Schelling, Hegel, Schopenhauer." See also Bradley, *English Poetry and German Philosophy,* Manchester, 1909; and J. W. Beach, *The Concept of Nature in Nineteenth-Century English Poetry* (New York, 1956), esp. p. 101.

influences. By itself, causal study always remains outside the central issue. It cannot explain elective affinities; it cannot explain why a man chose to be affected by one influence rather than another. In the present study I shall be concerned to understand a Weltanschauung from the inside, to grasp its inner coherence. My aim will be to show how its various components tend to hold together and support each other in an autonomous unity.

The impulse to undertake such a study arose from my unsuccessful attempt to understand Wordsworth's Immortality Ode. In a recent article T. M. Raysor discussed the "concepts" in that poem and frankly remarked, "I should be grateful to anyone who would undertake a complete analysis of such concepts in Wordsworth's cloudy and baffling metaphysical idealism." [8] Raysor, a very knowledgeable Wordsworthian, could make that remark after more than a century of studies in Wordsworth's "philosophy," for there has been, to my knowledge, no coherent analysis of Wordsworth's outlook as a whole, even though a holistic exposition might clarify much that is obscure in Wordsworth's poetry. However, as any student of Wordsworth will testify, it is very difficult to deduce the contours of Wordsworth's outlook from his poetry alone. And, like many scholars who have tried to fit Wordsworth's poetry into someone else's philosophical scheme, I thought that I might clarify Wordsworth's cloudy concepts by translating them into the idiom of German romantic philosophy.

I soon decided that this procedure was dangerous since poetry cannot justly be translated into philosophy. Each discipline follows its own special laws and conventions. But granted the force of this view, it may also be said that

8. T. M. Raysor, "The Themes of Immortality and Natural Piety in Wordsworth's Immortality Ode," *PMLA, 69* (1954), 861–2.

poetry and philosophy are separate only as disciplines. Both may spring from an identical Weltanschauung. The same person, for example, might be both philosopher and poet. On this point, a remark of Dilthey's is apropos: "Both philosophy and theology express a Weltanschauung based on actual, vital experience. The same is true of art, especially of literature. All three of them must ultimately correspond." [9] Of course, autonomous disciplines do exert a special influence on the outlooks of men who practice them, but on the whole Dilthey's remark is sound. A man does act in myriad compartments of life without losing his self-identity, without, that is, changing his Weltanschauung. As Jaspers puts it, "Philosophy . . . is simply the most differentiated, self-conscious expression for many, more widely scattered, less differentiated, yet actual Weltanschauungen." [1] By focusing my study on a common underlying Weltanschauung, I might, so I thought, validly illuminate both Wordsworth's poetry and German philosophy.

Limiting the discussion of German philosophy to the works of Schelling promised a gain in unity and depth. It also seemed clear that I would have to limit my materials from each writer to a period when his outlook remained stable and constant. As most scholars, notably de Selincourt, assert, Wordsworth began to change his attitudes sometime between 1805 and 1807.[2] Accordingly, all my Wordsworth citations will be taken from works composed in the period 1797–1805 (approximately the Great Decade). In Schelling's case, a shift began to occur around

9. *Wilhelm Diltheys Gesammelte Schriften,* ed. G. Misch et al. (8 vols. Leipzig and Berlin, Teubner, 1921–31), *8, 14.*
1. Karl Jaspers, *Psychologie der Weltanschauungen* (3d ed. Berlin, Springer, 1925), p. 10.
2. *The Prelude,* introd.

1806. That is the date for which Fuhrmans, Schelling's most useful commentator, has argued convincingly.[3] Schelling citations, then, are taken from works written during the period 1797–1806.

The very nature of my inquiry demanded that I should discuss exclusively traits common to the two writers. My object of interest was to be a historical Weltanschauung, not the complex personality of Wordsworth or Schelling taken singly. For my purposes, the great advantage of a comparative method is that it provides a way of isolating essential features. Since Wordsworth and Schelling did not influence one another, their common traits very likely reflect something essential in their outlook, for these correspondences cannot be explained as the results of a chance encounter. On the other hand, the traits not common to the two writers obviously would not represent necessary components in the basic structure of the outlook they shared.

One could argue that this kind of selectivity oversimplifies and misleads, since any analysis which leaves out distinctive details fails to describe adequately either author. This is, of course, true, but it is not here an important criticism since the analysis does not *pretend* to describe an individual mind. I mean only to describe holistically the essential features and the essential interrelationships of a Weltanschauung. This description is to serve as an orientation to more complex materials. As far as any individual author or work is concerned, the aim of the present study is primarily heuristic.

My procedure is one well established in psychology and sociology: that of typification. In descriptive psychology, for example, various traits of mind usually found occurring together are correlated by the psychologist in

3. Horst Fuhrmans, *Schellings Philosophie der Weltalter* (Düsseldorf, Schwann, 1954), p. 6, and passim.

order to disclose the basic pattern in a particular form of sanity or insanity. By correlating these essential features, the descriptive psychologist attempts to learn how a particular sort of mind functions. Such psychological typification is therefore employed not simply to classify minds; its primary function is to provide an insight into an individual mind in all its complexity. The psychologist realizes that the type is not the individual, but he also knows that an investigation of the type permits him to organize and clarify his investigation of the individuals who "belong" to the type.[4]

But the type concept as used by the psychologist is subtly different from the species concept used by the zoologist. The species is not simply a heuristic and descriptive idea but represents an actual genetic relationship among all the members who belong to it. The species *is* descriptive of the individual. Not so the type, which instead of describing the individual in its particularity simply points toward the individual. The central principle in the proper application of types is the principle *mutatis mutandis*. The investigator must always remind himself that his typological construction functions primarily as a guiding idea. This very fact, however, makes the type the intellectual tool par excellence for all idiographic study, that is, for all study which attempts to understand the personal or individual as such. In the present essay, then, I shall not attempt to describe a species of romanticism but shall attempt to construct a type of romantic outlook. Such a type may function as a guiding idea, which permits the student to examine minutely an individual mind in all its complexity without losing sight of the whole.

4. See E. Kretschmer, "Der Typus als erkenntnistheoretisches Problem," in *Studium Generale, 4* (1951), 399–402. An excellent general discussion may be found in Eugen Seiterich, *Die logische Struktur des Typusbegriffes,* Freiburg im Bresgau, 1930.

Roughly speaking, there are three ways in which a Weltanschauung type may be constructed by a comparative method, and I shall list them in order of increasing usefulness. The first, and most common, way I call extrinsic typification because it attempts to characterize a Weltanschauung in the idiom of a different one. By comparing Wordsworth and Whitehead, for example, I might describe Wordsworth's "feeling for nature as exhibiting entwined prehensive unities, each suffused with modal presences of others." [5] Whitehead's unusual language makes it specially clear that the characterization is more descriptive of Whitehead than of Wordsworth. Whitehead's categories are constitutive; they lend a special flavor to that which is being described, a flavor extrinsic to Wordsworth. This subtle distortion would characterize any attempt to describe Wordsworth's Weltanschauung in the idiom of Spinoza's philosophy, or Plato's, or indeed in any idiom which expressed a Weltanschauung qualitatively different from Wordsworth's own.

The second method, that of neutral or abstract typification, attempts to avoid the problem of distortion by characterizing a type of mind in a neutral idiom. Using this method I might say that Wordsworth and Whitehead both exhibit a tendency to perceive a simultaneous fusion and separation of subject and object, object and object. Every object is sensed as being at once subject and object. For what it is worth, such an idiom of description attempts to avoid imposing its own metaphysical or cultural coloration. But in this attempt it is not and cannot be altogether successful, since *all* terms have philosophical and cultural implications and tend to color what they describe. Yet, terms like subject and object are *relatively* noncommittal, and it is possible by using them to identify not only

5. A. N. Whitehead's own description of Wordsworth, in *Science and the Modern World* (New York, Macmillan, 1925), p. 122.

Wordsworth and Whitehead but a long list of names from Thales to Bergson as displaying the same basic mental structure. Stallknecht alone has pointed out that Wordsworth's outlook is analogous not only to those of Whitehead and Schelling but also to those of Plotinus, Bruno, Böhme, Spinoza, Kant, and others.[6] Undoubtedly he is right, but surely on a very abstract level. Indeed, on this level of abstraction one discovers that human history can offer but three or four basic types of Weltanschauung. Such abstract types are, of course, useful in a preliminary and tentative way, but they inevitably leave out essential components, since a Weltanschauung is never a pure structure but is always essentially colored by its special, culturally conditioned categories and assumptions. The most carefully neutral description remains, by virtue of its very neutrality, extrinsic.

The third method, that of intrinsic typification, is more genuinely descriptive and therefore more useful heuristically. Because categories are inevitably constitutive (a fact recognized by every literary critic who insists that meaning and expression are inseparable), intrinsic typification attempts to characterize a Weltanschauung as far as possible in its own historic idiom. Dilthey has been criticized for subsuming all Weltanschauungen under three abstract types; yet, ironically, it was Dilthey who never tired of insisting that human consciousness is constituted by culture, *essentially* conditioned by history.[7] Any typification, therefore, ought to be descriptive of this essential historicity. In fact, Dilthey recognized this and considered his abstract types only to be indispensable preliminary

6. N. P. Stallknecht has gathered most of his discussion of Wordsworth's philosophy in *Strange Seas of Thought*, Durham, Duke Univ. Press, 1945.

7. See, e.g., *Gesammelte Schriften, 8*, 38: "denn man stösst hier eben an die Geschichtlichkeit des menschlichen Bewusstseins als eine Grundeigenschaft desselben."

tools. In this he was, I think, correct, for just as the intrinsic type is a guiding idea for understanding the individual, an abstract type remains a guiding idea in the construction of an intrinsic type. In Chapter 2, I sketch for
the reader the abstract structure of the Weltanschauung
common to Wordsworth and Schelling. In subsequent
chapters, however, the description is genuinely intrinsic,
since the two figures being compared shared the same
historical outlook which they commonly expressed in
terms like "Life," "Nature," and "Imagination." In my
analysis I shall keep to this historic idiom as far as this is
consonant with clarity and comprehensibility.

If the principle *mutatis mutandis* is kept in mind, I
think it will be found that the type of Weltanschauung
I describe is characteristic of nineteenth-century writers
other than Wordsworth and Schelling.[8] Some figures
traditionally called romantics may not, of course, bear a
fundamental resemblance to the type, but that may simply
signify that they ought not to be called romantics. It is
not sufficient to identify romantics by isolated traits. Every
definition of romanticism which merely lists an array of
clearly identifiable characteristics has proved inadequate,
not because "romanticism" is meaningless but because
spiritual similarities do not always express themselves by
similar external characteristics. A meaningful definition of
a spiritual movement must embrace the spiritual, subjective realm and not limit itself merely to the precipitates
of subjectivity.

However, I am not mainly interested in historical
definitions but in textual interpretation, where typological
study may be helpful in an oblique, but significant, way.

8. See Spranger, "Theorie des Verstehens," p. 372: "In der Formel
mutatis mutandis steckt dann das wesentlichste Rätsel des Verstehens. Schon
hier aber deutet sich an, dass wir das Seelische nur verstehen durch das
Geistige hindurch."

One form of the type concept, the genre, has always been used in textual study. More than once, of course, the genre has been thought of as a genuine species, and this has some justification when the genre is truly genetic, when it represents the scheme of conventions under which the text was composed. But all too often the abstract genre is considered to be a real entity which helps define a fictive amalgamation like the "realm of literature." So used, the genre concept helps propagate the illusion that there is a unified body of texts whose character may be penetrated by the application of a priori laws and techniques. If, however, textual interpretation is conceived to be an idiographic discipline, the genre properly functions as a guiding idea about general formal aims. As such, it acts as a wedge into the actual, complex, particular formal aims of the individual text.

A Weltanschauung type may have a similar function whenever the text does not provide sufficient clues to the direction of its meaning. A grasp of the author's type of outlook provides the reader with a clue as to the text's purport. I know of no significant poetic or philosophical text that does not have its cruxes, and there is no better way to discover the probable meaning of many cruxes than to refer them to the author's characteristic view of things. When one is confronted with a problematical passage, capable of being construed plausibly in different ways, it is helpful to adopt sympathetically the author's type of outlook in order to determine which meaning is the most typical and probable. This is helpful, of course, even when one is not aware that a problem of interpretation exists, since certainty in textual interpretation is impossible and an uncritical sense of certainty is automatically suspect. Weltanschauung analysis may therefore serve the same purpose as philological investigation. Both may be used for the systematic verification of an interpretation. In the final chapter, where I discuss the Immortality Ode in detail, I shall attempt to resolve cruxes in that poem by invoking the poet's typical attitudes as they are defined in the previous chapters. This final discussion will, I hope, demonstrate that a type construct, used flexibly, can be helpful in penetrating textual meaning.

2. The Structure of Experience

THE PATTERN OF EXPERIENCE shared by Wordsworth and
Schelling I call "Enthusiasm." This word, which I have
borrowed from Jaspers, seems preferable, even with its
unfortunate connotations, to the word romanticism.[1] I
prefer to say Enthusiasm and mean romanticism than to
say romanticism and run the risk of raising antipathy
and confusion. Lovejoy has done his work too well. Be-
sides this, I have no right to claim a larger application for
my description before its wider relevance is demonstrated.
In any case, Enthusiasm, as I use the term, does not have
its modern pejorative connotations but remains much
closer to its root meaning: possessed by a god. The term
does imply an optimistic and fervid outlook, but this has
little in common with the impetuous and impermanent
fervor the Germans call *Schwärmerei*. Enthusiasm implies
a constant and sober way of confronting reality. There is
no jumping from object to object in order to enjoy rapture
for its own sake. It is a consistent and disciplined, yet
highly affirmative way of experiencing things.

One basic pattern underlies all of Enthusiasm's experi-

1. Cf. Karl Jaspers, "Die enthusiastische Einstellung," in *Psychologie der
Weltanschauungen*, pp. 119–37. I am indebted to Jaspers' analysis for
some of the ideas in the present chapter.

ence. It might be called the pattern of mutual inclusiveness. To state the matter in purely abstract form, Enthusiasm opposes the notion that A is not Not-A. At one and the same time A is *both* A *and* Not-A. Everything belongs with and implies its other. At first glance, it would seem that Enthusiasm would be much concerned with paradox and, as a matter of fact, many of Enthusiasm's expressions seem highly paradoxical. However, Enthusiasm passes over its necessary paradoxes and focuses attention upon the ultimate reconciliation of things. It does so because it always senses a beyond in reference to which the apparent distinctions between things are overcome. It is the beyond which makes A equal Not-A, not the paradoxical nature of the entities in themselves. It is the beyond which gives Enthusiasm its bright confidence and high expectancy.

On the surface, this pattern may seem very similar to mysticism with its denial of all distinctions. Sometimes, indeed, Enthusiasm may experience a mystical fusion with the beyond, but this is merely a moment within its experience as a whole. It is a necessary moment, one that sustains Enthusiasm's confidence and expectancy, but in the general course of experience the beyond remains unattained. The subject is always faced with distinctions *to be* overcome, distinctions like that between life and death, the ideal and the real. Yet, at the same time, the task of overcoming distinctions is already implicitly accomplished by the beyond. The both-and motif underlies every aspect of experience.

Enthusiasm, then, differs from mysticism in that it preserves a separation from its object. Except for rare mystical moments, the Enthusiast always has a sense of his own selfhood. Yet the distinction between the self and its object has a special character; it is at once separation *and* fusion. Subject and object do not exist in different strata of being but belong to the same essential reality. The subject feels a deep kinship with his object, and the relationship between them can be called a kind of love. There is an awareness of separateness in the relationship and, at the same time, a sense of identity.

Keats described the relationship better, perhaps, than anyone else when he spoke of "fellowship with essence." Subject and object are distinct, yet they have a deep kinship with one another because they both belong to the same essence of things. In Wordsworth and Schelling, this motif is omnipresent. "The external world," said Schelling, "lies open before us in order that we may find again in it the history of our own spirit." And he wrote of the "inner love and kinship which we bear to nature." [2] In like manner, Wordsworth spoke of the "analogy betwixt The mind of man and nature," and he looked

> with feelings of fraternal love
> Upon those unassuming things, that hold
> A silent station in this beauteous world.[3]

Because the subject is not radically different from his object neither has a preferential status. Humanness is thingness and vice versa. Wordsworth once spoke of the "human Soul of universal earth," and felt that

> deeply drinking in the soul of things
> We shall be wise perforce.[4]

The poet always abjured those purely human concerns which eclipse "the impersonated thought." [5] Wordsworth's poetry is at once highly subjective and highly impersonal, and these characteristics are ultimately identical, since

2. *1*, 383; 7, 62.
3. Verse fragment, see *The Prelude*, p. 600; *The Prelude*, XII, 50–2.
4. Prospectus to *The Excursion*, l. 84; *The Ruined Cottage*, ll. 92–3, *5*, 402.
5. *The Prelude*, VIII, 646.

they both spring from the sense of kinship between man and thing.

When Schelling proclaimed the *Ichheit* of all things, he was being no more a solipsist than Wordsworth was being when he approved "the impersonated thought." On the contrary, Schelling was denying that reality can be interpreted in purely human terms. With passionate irony, he attacked Fichte's limitation of ego to the I of human consciousness.[6] For Schelling, ego is "simultaneously subjective and objective being."[7] The external world has the same character which the internal world has; that is the very point which the *System of Transcendental Idealism* sets out to demonstrate, and it is the core of the *Identitätsphilosophie*. The philosophy of nature and the philosophy of consciousness are to be brought together, not by asserting, as Kant had done, that reality for us is a product of consciousness but by asserting that mind and the objective world have ultimately the same character. The early works of both Schelling and Hegel passionately attempt to overcome the purely human limitations spelled out in Kant's epistemology. Hegel characterized his whole system as an attempt to demonstrate substance as subject,[8] and this doctrine parallels Wordsworth's notion that humanness is thingness and vice versa.

Despite its confidence in ultimate fusion, Enthusiasm does sense a kind of separation between man and thing, but it always tries to show that the separation is not fundamental and that it can be overcome. The bête noire of Enthusiasm is estrangement; it fights against all "disconnection dead and spiritless";[9] it pits all its energy against

6. See especially 7, 3–126.
7. *4*, 289.
8. Cf. Hegel, *The Phenomenology of Mind,* trans. J. B. Baillie (2d ed. London, Allen & Unwin, 1931), pp. 80, 85, 97.
9. *The Ruined Cottage,* l. 62, *5*, 402.

any radical separation of things. Kant's *Ding an sich* was insupportable to the early idealists, and they made it the center of philosophical discussion.[1] They flatly rejected all doctrines which held that mind and the physical world belong to different strata of reality. Both Leibnitz and Kant were wrong. Schelling reproached the Kantian by saying that for him the "world and all reality is fundamentally foreign to our spirit." Kant is the devil's advocate; he leaves us "lonely and forsaken amidst the world, surrounded everywhere by spectres."[2]

It was this kind of separation which Wordsworth also strove to overcome. He denied that there was a separate, purely human realm with purely human concerns. For him the countryside was valuable in itself but it was primarily valuable because there the human realm and physical reality truly come together. His poetry focuses on the juxtaposition of man and nature, not on nature alone. There is always a human figure as part of the landscape, although it may simply be the poet himself. Even then it is not simply the scene which the poet describes but also himself as part of the scene. The effect is that of a fellowship between man and nature, between the human and nonhuman. Wordsworth devotes a special section of his poetry to "Poems on the Naming of Places," commemorating, so to speak, the joining of the two realms. It is because the "infant Babe" is no Kantian that he is "bless'd":

> No outcast he, bewilder'd and depress'd;
> Along his infant veins are interfus'd
> The gravitation and the filial bond
> Of nature, that connect him with the world.[3]

1. Nicolai Hartmann, *Die Philosophie des deutschen Idealismus, I Teil* (Berlin and Leipzig, de Gruÿter, 1923), p. 7: "Das Ding an sich wurde der zentrale Gegenstand philosophischer Diskussion in den nächstfolgenden Jahren."
2. *1*, 360, 362.
3. *The Prelude*, II, 261–4.

The child and the world are not fused but interfused. Reciprocity is the fundamental characteristic of the subject-object relationship. Neither the self nor the object loses its self-identity in the relationship, yet the two are joined through a process of "interfusion." The interfusion occurs because both sides have the same essence; subject and object engage in a loving dialectic. Fusion in separation or interfusion is precisely reciprocity, and reciprocity characterizes Wordsworth's own description of subject and object. For him the mind is "fitted" to the external world and

> Theme this but little heard of among men—
> The external World is fitted to the Mind.[4]

A thing is not "out there," to itself and inaccessible; by the very similarity of its nature to our own, it strikes a responsive chord within us. Yet the object is not simply "in us" exclusively. It is both "out there" and "in us" at one and the same time. By the logic of both-and, Enthusiasm preserves the distinction between mind and thing.

> If consciousness were something absolutely inward and no unmediated contact between it and outward things could be conceived, we would find that we do not at all see things outside of us . . . but that we simply see them in ourselves. If this were so, there could be no possible separation between inner and outer worlds. The outer world would dissolve completely in the inner. And since inner is only distinguishable in contrast to outer, the inner along with the outer world would unavoidably collapse.[5]

Estrangement is conquered not by fusion but by reciprocity.

4. Prospectus to *The Excursion*, ll. 67–8.
5. Schelling, *1*, 390–1.

The reciprocity of subject and object is a true one, for both sides actively participate. Each side gives and receives, so that the process itself is simultaneously one of activity and passivity. For Schelling, the highest moment of being is the union of "utmost passivity with limitless activity," and he speaks of "an activity peaceful as the deepest calm, and a calmness active as the highest activity." [6] This is the very quality which the subject possesses when he engages in a reciprocal relationship with external things. For Wordsworth, that is nature's "glory":

> From nature doth emotion come, and moods
> Of calmness equally are nature's gift,
> This is her glory; these two attributes
> Are sister horns that constitute her strength;
> This twofold influence is the sun and shower
> Of all her bounties, both in origin
> And end alike benignant. Hence it is,
> That Genius which exists by interchange
> Of peace and excitation, finds in her
> His best and purest Friend, from her receives
> That energy by which he seeks the truth,
> Is rouz'd, aspires, grasps, struggles, wishes, craves,
> From her that happy stillness of the mind
> Which fits him to receive it, when unsought. [7]

The relationship between mind and object is active and reciprocal; even when one side is passive the other is active, so that the union of activity and passivity occurs within an active process, in the same way that fusion occurs within a condition of separation.

When the experience is looked at from the side of the subject, this active reciprocity of subject and object is

6. *1*, 324–5; *4*, 305.

7. *The Prelude*, XII, 1–14. Note also a similar pronouncement in *The Recluse*, ll. 292–6, *5*, 324.

sensed as fulfillment in striving. The subject actively "aspires, grasps, struggles, wishes, craves," and he also receives "that happy stillness of the mind." But even this happy stillness occurs within a process. Enthusiasm is almost always in movement; it always has a beyond toward which it bends. Schelling said of the mind that "it seeks itself, but even in doing so flees from itself," [8] and Wordsworth said that the soul

> retains an obscure sense
> Of possible sublimity, to which,
> With growing faculties she doth aspire,
> With faculties still growing, feeling still
> That whatsoever point they gain, they still
> Have something to pursue.[9]

Typically, even in the process of seeking, Enthusiasm senses fulfillment, just as it unites with its object by the process of reciprocity. The patterns are precisely analogous because they are reflections of one another. Unity with the object *is* fulfillment.

Such unity is fulfillment because the object with which Enthusiasm interacts is presented in a special way; it is imbedded, so to speak, in the beyond. Unity with the object is a kind of unity with the beyond, for the reciprocal process itself evokes a sense of "something far more deeply interfused" which dwells in all things, in

> the round ocean, and the living air
> And the blue sky, and in the mind of man.

The beyond is something that subsists within the subject and his object and also beyond them both. Subject and object are unified because of an essence which "rolls

8. *3*, 489.
9. *The Prelude*, II, 336–41.

through all things." They are akin because they both belong to a greater totality. This totality is apprehended in the object, but it is never fully given in experience; it always reaches beyond, always stretches out toward the "light of setting suns." In the section of "Tintern Abbey" from which these phrases are taken, the word "all" occurs six times in five lines (101–5) and fifteen times between lines 40 and 133. The mind and things are akin because they belong to an infinite totality which unites them.

Because the object is imbedded in an infinite totality, active striving for unity with the object is also striving toward possible sublimity. But the unity is in a sense achieved by the reciprocal process itself. The sense of possible sublimity is also a sense of actual sublimity:

> Our destiny, our nature, and our home
> Is with infinitude, and only there;
> With hope it is, hope that can never die,
> Effort, and expectation, and desire,
> And something evermore about to be.[1]

Infinitude is not only something held before the subject, a beyond never reached; it is also his nature and his home. His hope can never die; what is evermore about to be is also something ever present. Striving never ceases, but in striving itself man fulfills his nature.

For this reason, Enthusiasm is highly affirmative. In the very process of striving it is constantly realizing value. Since the beyond is *both* in experience *and* always just out of reach, everything is presently good and beautiful, even that goodness and beauty which is still to be realized. The character of the subject-object relationship sustains hope and expectation and desire; all oppositions are reconciled in something evermore about to be. The distinctions are

1. *The Prelude*, VI, 538–42.

not completely overcome in experience; there is always a task, but Enthusiasm strives with the confidence that its task will ultimately be fulfilled, for in experience itself it senses that the task is being fulfilled.

Although Enthusiasm looks before and after and pines for what is not, it does so because of the value in that which is. The beyond is in two places at once, and therefore the entire experience is characterized by the both-and pattern. The striving toward a beyond is at the same time an affirmation of the here and now. The process itself is valuable: "The direct goal of nature in the process I have just described is simply the process itself." "Existence," said Schelling, "is self-affirmation, and self-affirmation is existence. The one has precisely the same meaning as the other." [2] And Wordsworth's "sentiment of being" was fundamentally

> the deep enthusiastic joy,
> The rapture of the Hallelujah sent
> From all that breathes and is.[3]

Enthusiasm's loving reciprocity with things directly reflects an infinite and loving totality to which subject and object both belong. The beyond reconciles all things in a great self-affirmation, and the subject, along with every aspect of his experience, participates in that affirmation.

> If, therefore, thou hast seen the fullness of existence, as it is for itself, without measure or goal, then thou shouldst also know the inner and holy bond between things and how among themselves, through the unity of the essence to which they belong, they become one.[4]

This I take to be the common structure of experience in Wordsworth and Schelling. In subsequent chapters, I shall

2. 2, 514; 7, 53.
3. *The Prelude*, XIII, 261–3.
4. Schelling, 7, 201.

try to describe the quality of that experience in relation to the ideas and categories which actually sustained it. In the course of the exposition, as the structure gathers more substance, the coherence of the interrelationships ought to become clearer.

3. God and the World

ENTHUSIASM IS FUNDAMENTALLY a religious experience; the beyond which it constantly senses is nothing other than God Himself. God's essence infuses subject and object, giving both a deep kinship with one another, yet God always seems to lie beyond subject and object as such. Enthusiasm is constantly striving to reach the beyond so that it may fuse with "God who is our home," but only rarely does it fully attain this goal. Nevertheless, even in so striving, the Enthusiast feels himself to be quite literally possessed by God. The least of things in experience evokes an "undersense of greatest." Everything has a shimmer of divinity, yet this shimmer points to something which is still to be realized. The actual glory of experience provides a motivation to achieve something even more glorious. The Enthusiast feels himself to be God's agent; he has sight of God's purpose and consciously tries to realize it.

Wordsworth sought to realize the divine purpose by teaching the truth of his vision to the readers of his poetry. The prophetic impulse lies behind much of his verse, as Legouis pointed out: "When every man shall possess the poet's eye, the poet's ear, the poet's heart, that millennium, so fondly looked for in other paths of progress, will have been reached indeed. A distant end, no doubt, but one towards which every step is a delight." [1] In striving toward the distant goal, every step is a delight; that is the character of Wordsworth's prophecy. Wordsworth's great philosophic poem, said Coleridge, "was to infer and reveal the proof of, and necessity for, the whole state of man and society being subject to, and illustrative of, a redemptive process in operation, showing how this idea reconciled all the anomalies, and promised future glory and restoration." [2] The poet himself, like the little child in the Immortality Ode, is a "mighty prophet" and a "seer blest":

> I was a chosen Son.
> For hither I had come with holy powers
> And faculties. [3]

Schelling also thought of himself as a prophet. In 1805 he wrote to Windischmann, "I join hands with you in an eternal covenant for that which is our mutual religion: the embodiment of the divine in science, life, and art, and the universal propagation and establishment of the same in the minds and hearts of men." "Philosophy is the science of the divine"; it is to bring about a recognition "of the divinity of nature and the great unity of all being." In the light of the new teaching, "all will become unified and one even in science and knowledge, as from eternity everything has always been unified in being and in the life of nature." [4]

In both Schelling and Wordsworth the prophecy for the future points to a glorious redemption which is taking place in the present. Wordsworth's poem was to show "a

1. Émile Legouis, *The Early Life of William Wordsworth*, trans. J. W. Matthews (New York, 1897), p. 5.

2. S. T. Coleridge, *Table Talk*, July 31, 1832; quoted by Darbishire in Wordsworth, 5, 364.

3. *The Prelude*, III, 82–4.

4. G. L. Plitt, *Aus Schellings Leben in Briefen* (3 vols. Leipzig, Hirzel, 1869–70), 2, 73. Schelling, 7, 30, 126.

redemptive process in operation," and Schelling's philosophy was to reveal the divinity and unity of that which "has always been unified and one." Every step is a delight because every step is a realization of something which is still to be realized. The religious prophecy speaks of the coming redemption as something which is already implicitly achieved. God will redeem the world because God is already carrying out the redemptive process in the actual world.

Thus, the New Jerusalem is coming to be, here and now in this beauteous world:

> Not in Utopia, subterraneous Fields,
> Or some secreted Island, Heaven knows where,
> But in the very world which is the world
> Of all of us, the place in which, in the end,
> We find our happiness, or not at all.[5]

There is no world beyond this one, nor is there any need for another, for this world is itself divine. Enthusiasm has a pantheistic flavor. "There is only one world . . ." said Schelling, "one universe in which all is glorious, truly divine, and beautiful." Here "the smallest is as holy as the greatest," because the world as such is holy.[6] Wordsworth mused, as he contemplated the vale of Grasmere, "they who are dwellers in this holy place Must needs themselves be hallowed." And Wordsworth's vale is not only holy, not just a parcel of divinity; it is also perfect and autonomous:

> A Whole without dependence or defect,
> Made for itself; and happy in itself,
> Perfect Contentment, Unity entire.[7]

The goal of the world is simply self-affirmation. ("Existenz ist Selbstbejahung.") The pantheistic flavor of such ideas

---

5. *The Prelude*, X, 724–8.
6. *4*, 314 (also, *5*, 276: "Est ist nur eine Welt"); *7*, 189.
7. *The Recluse*, ll. 277–8, *5*, 323; ll. 149–51, *5*, 318.

is even more apparent when Wordsworth, still gazing at his
vale, exclaims, "this majestic self-sufficing world, This all
in all of nature." [8]

Such outbursts lend force to the hypothesis that Wordsworth and Schelling were pantheists, yet there are other
expressions which work against the thesis. Wordsworth, for
example, spoke of

> the one
> Surpassing Life, which out of space and time,
> Nor touched by welterings of passion, is
> And hath the name of God.[9]

And Schelling said that "God is the eternal night when He
is alone in Himself." [1] Wordsworth and Schelling cannot
be called outright pantheists because they sense, with all
their glorification of things, a God who is beyond the
world itself. The term "panentheism" comes to mind, and
such a label might be defensible, for it overcomes the
radical distinction between "transcendence" and "immanence." Schelling once remarked impatiently, "When
will people finally come to see that in my doctrine . . .
both 'immanence' and 'transcendence' are completely
empty words?" [2] In an admirable attempt at precision,
Horst Fuhrmans has coined the phrase "Immanence-
Theism" to describe Schelling's religious doctrine.[3] Dean
Inge, with even more precision, has called Wordsworth's
religion "pantheistic mysticism," and, significantly, Inge's
definition echoes a term which Dilthey has applied to the
early religious views of Hegel, namely, "der mystische
Pantheismus." [4] "Panentheism," "Immanence-Theism,"

8. Ibid., variant (MS) version.
9. *The Prelude*, VI, 154–7.
1. 7, 162, cited in Fuhrmans, p. 59.
2. 2, 377.
3. Fuhrmans, p. 63.
4. W. R. Inge, *Studies of English Mystics* (London, Murray, 1906), p. 178;
Dilthey, *Gesammelte Schriften, 4,* 138–58.

"pantheistic mysticism" are all helpful terms, which point
accurately to one aspect of Enthusiasm's religious experience. But these terms should be qualified if they are to be
descriptive of the religious experience as a whole.

Inge said that in pantheistic mysticism "God is really
everything; while in ordinary pantheism everything is
God." [5] The pantheist senses himself and his world as
coextensive with the being of God, whereas the mystical
pantheist has a sense of fusion both with the world and
with a God beyond the world. The mystical pantheist is
merged both with God and with things. From time to time,
Wordsworth described such occasions in his poetry:

> Oh 'tis a joy divine on summer days
> When not a breeze is stirring, not a cloud,
> To sit within some solitary wood,
> Far in some lonely wood, and hear no sound
> Which the heart does not make, or else so fit[s]
> To its own temper that in external things
> No longer seem internal difference
> All melts away, and things that are without
> Live in our minds as in their native home. [6]

Schelling called such fusion "intellectual perception"; and
he thought of it as the highest moment of being. In such
moments "the perceiving or intuiting self is identical with
that which he perceives." [7]

In his mystical moment, the Enthusiast seems to merge
both with a God who is "out of space and time" and with
a world which is present to his physical senses. Such an
experience is possible because the transcendent God is not
sensed as an "up there" but as an "out here." The soul
fuses with a beyond that rolls through nature.

5. *Studies of English Mystics*, p. 178.
6. Verse fragment, 5, 343.
7. *1*, 319.

When strongly breath'd upon
By this sensation, whencesoe'er it comes
Of union or communion doth the soul
Rejoice as in her highest joy: for there,
There chiefly, hath she feeling whence she is,
And, passing through all Nature rests with God.[8]

The mind passes through the world, across the horizon-bounded ocean, toward the light of setting suns, so that when the mind truly merges with God it merges with things as well. God is a totality that includes things, as Inge pointed out. In the moment of mystic fusion the Enthusiast is at one with God and the world. God no longer stretches out beyond nature in the light of setting suns, but seems to weld the whole statically, like the sun in its meridian height. The Enthusiast senses that all things

Are god, Existing in the mighty whole,
As indistinguishable as the cloudless East
At noon is from the cloudless west, when all
The hemisphere is one cerulean blue.[9]

"Mystical pantheism" is an accurate term for such an experience, but it is a term which describes only one moment in Enthusiasm's religious experience as a whole. The mystic is fulfilled only in the moment of fusion; the Enthusiast is fulfilled in striving for fusion. It is true that the mystical moment may constitute Enthusiasm's most complete fulfillment, but it is a moment which is rarely attained and which quickly disappears. In the general course of experience, the Enthusiast senses his separation from things and, therefore, from God. Such separation is the wellspring of his incessant striving, and the moment of mystical fusion is a vanishing point which lends a con-

8. *The Prelude,* VIII, 830–5.
9. *The Prelude,* fragment, p. 512–3.

fident tone to the process of striving as such. Only rarely is the hemisphere one cerulean blue; most often the infinite unity of all things dwells in the light of setting suns.

Throughout his writings in *Naturphilosophie,* Schelling made a distinction which is of first importance for an understanding of Enthusiasm's religious experience. He distinguished "between nature as she appears (i.e. mere *natura naturata,* nature in her particularization and separation from the whole, a mere reflection of the Absolute) and nature in herself, as merged with the Absolute, the infinite Being-affirmed of God." [1] Nature herself is in both cases the same, but Schelling has made a distinction between two modes of apprehending nature. In one mode— that of mystical, pantheistic fusion—nature is the divine totality; in the other mode, nature can be distinguished both from ourselves and from a transcendent God. Enthusiasm tends to recognize both modes at the same time, just as Schelling did. Immediately before saying that all beings "are god" and exist in one unified totality, Wordsworth had said "all beings live with god." Neither mode of apprehending nature exists by itself, even though they are distinct from one another. Enthusiasm preserves both modes at the same time, as complements of one another. The divine, creative independence of the world is the gift of a separate Godhood, and the very nature of the transcendent God is felt to be complemented by the nature of the world. God and the world are both separate and, somehow, together.

However, the togetherness of God and the world is not effected by the agency of a *tertium quid* like Providence in the Neoplatonic cosmology. Schelling was insistent on this point: "From infinite to finite—no transition! This was a principle of the oldest philosophy. . . . Only in later periods did spiritless systems seek to find middle members

1. 5, 378. The distinction was borrowed, of course, from Spinoza.

between infinity and finitude." [2] But, if God is both immanent and transcendent and if there is no mediation between infinity and finitude, how can God's nature be expressed adequately? That was for Schelling, as a philosopher, the great problem. His philosophy, said Fuhrmans,
"was almost from the beginning a wrestling with the
relationship of absolute to finite being, of God to world." [3]
Nor is it surprising that Schelling and Wordsworth should
provide analogous expressions for this relationship, for the
pattern of their expressions is implicit in the structure of
their experience.

God gives himself to the world; the divine shimmer of
things is "given by God." [4] It is God's giving which makes
the world glorious, and God's transcendence is preserved
"precisely in order to give an unambiguous accent to the
world." [5] The ideal and divine qualities in things come
from God:

> Wisdom and Spirit of the universe!
> Thou Soul that art the eternity of thought!
> That giv'st to forms and images a breath
> And everlasting motion! [6]

It is God's transcendence which causes the world itself to
have extraterrestrial qualities. If the being of the world
and the being of God were equated, then, for Enthusiasm,
the dignity of both would suffer, not just the dignity of
God as theistic opponents of pantheism complain. God's
separateness guarantees the ideality of the world. If God
were exclusively thingness, whence would come the beyond, the sense sublime, the infinite shimmer of things?
Things are, in fact, divine, but divinity is a property which

2. *1*, 367–8.
3. Fuhrmans, p. 6.
4. "Tribute," l. 28, *4*, 79.
5. Fuhrmans, p. 20.
6. *The Prelude*, I, 428–31.

is conferred upon them by a loving God beyond thingness. "The speaking face of earth" is suffused with ideality; it is a "bodily Image" which has a "soul divine." [7] This ideality is not simply another attribute of a universal substance; it is a quality which is sought and given, which is special and glorious and, at the same time, universal.

Wordsworth apostrophized, "Great God! Who send'st thyself into this breathing world." [8] God sends Himself into the world because reality is good. Like the Enthusiast, God says yes to reality. "Thou art pleased, Pleased with thy crags and woody steeps," said Wordsworth of Grasmere, and he expresses God's own affirmation of the real world.[9] God, said Schelling, is "the infinite affirmation of himself," and the world is "the infinite Being-affirmed of God." God realizes Himself in the world, his world and ours. Schelling thought of the world as the objective expression of God's subjective affirmation. "The act of subject-objectification goes through all things, and transmits itself to all particular forms, which, since they are only different appearances of the general and unconditioned, are, in this, themselves unconditioned." By God's agency, "the inner of all things . . . is the unity of real and ideal." [1] The ideal God affirms Himself in real things, and therefore the meanest flower that blows is holy.

The world is God's affirmative self-realization. Without the world, God would be incomplete because He would not be real. There is only one reality: this world, our world; and ideality only achieves its true being in partnership with reality, just as reality only becomes divine in partnership with ideality. The world, as reality, is a necessary counterpart of God. God and the world are not

7. *The Prelude*, V, 12–16.
8. *The Prelude*, X, 386–7.
9. *The Recluse*, ll. 117–8, 5, 317.
1. 5, 374, 377, 325; 7, 189.

equated, but they are separate in Enthusiasm's special way. There is "a mutual implication of subject and object, of God's being and the being of the world." [2] God's relationship to the world is analogous to Enthusiasm's relationship to its object, at once affirmative and loving and mutually self-fulfilling. Yet it is not a relationship of complete fusion; because a separate God realizes Himself through the world, all things are *partners* in a glorious task. All things strive toward God, for God is fulfilling Himself through things. All the world is kin; everything has "fellowship with essence."

Fellowship with essence is the characteristic religious theme of Wordsworth's poetry. The mind of the child, for example, reflects what Schelling called the subject-objectification that goes through all things. The child's mind,

> Even as an agent of the one great mind,
> Creates, creator and receiver both,
> Working but in alliance with the works
> Which it beholds.[3]

From the loving reciprocity between the one great mind and the works which it beholds comes to the Enthusiast

> the sense
> Of majesty, and beauty, and repose,
> A blended holiness of earth and sky.[4]

Without such blending, there would be no majesty; earth would have no holiness, and holiness no reality. This same sort of blending occurred when "the sweet breath of Heaven" blew against the poet's body. It was because he felt externally the "breath of God" that he "felt within A corresponding mild creative breeze." [5] Only from the

2. Fuhrmans, p. 42.
3. *The Prelude*, II, 272-5.
4. *The Recluse*, ll. 142-4, 5, 318.
5. *The Prelude*, V, 222; I, 41-3.

"blended might" of earth and heaven can come the sense sublime. Wordsworth felt that sublimity when he contemplated the vale of Grasmere:

> How goodly, how exceeding fair, how pure
> From all reproach is yon ethereal vault,
> And this deep Vale its earthly counterpart,
> By which, and under which, we are enclosed.[6]

These lines express in concrete terms Wordsworth's characteristic religious view. Earth and heaven are counterparts; they are essentially akin to one another, but not equated. But God's separateness is also nearness. Earth and heaven work "in alliance." God and the world are never completely without each other, and together within God's totality they are partners in a glorious and holy self-affirmation.

The holy self-affirmation is only here on earth, for only here exists the blended holiness of the real and the ideal. Beyond the earth there is no other reality. Therefore, Wordsworth worshiped "among the depths of things." God reveals Himself only in His works:

> In such access of mind, in such high hour
> Of visitation from the living God,
> He did not feel the God; he felt his works.[7]

"Here and only here is God revealed and present, and He unveils himself to him who is open to things." [8]

Revelation is a perception of the actual unity and divinity of the world, for the world itself is "God in the reality of His life and His self-revelation." [9] By striving to unite with the things of the world, man is striving toward God.

---

6. *The Recluse*, ll. 640–3, 5, 334–5.
7. *The Ruined Cottage*, ll. 134–6, 5, 382.
8. Fuhrmans, p. 44.
9. Schelling, 7, 59.

Union with the world means union (not fusion) with God, for then we join the divine fellowship which is everywhere realizing God's purposes. Revelation is therefore redemption. The true state of things is revealed. Man, along with everything else in the world, is redeemed; he belongs to the divine totality. Wordsworth spoke of the "pervading grace That hath been, is, and shall be," because he knew that God and the world are eternally in active partnership, and that they will attain the ultimate goal.

> it shall be my pride
> That I have dared to tread this holy ground,
> Speaking no dream but things oracular,
> Matter not lightly to be heard by those
> Who to the letter of the outward promise
> Do read the invisible soul.[1]

1. *The Prelude*, XII, 43–4, 250–5.

4. The Life of Things

*He who rightly sees God's presence in the life of all
things, who tries to understand God as above, and
through, and in all things, who begins in himself to
know himself, and holds up to his own nature other
animated things, will at length discern in animals,
plants, and stones, a single uniform life.*[1]

FOR ENTHUSIASM, everything is alive.[2] "The positive principle of life," says Schelling, "is spread through the entire
creation, and penetrates each individual being as the com-

1. F. C. Oetinger, *Die Philosophie der Alten* (2 vols. Leipzig, Cotta,
1762) 2, p. 31.
2. For a discussion of panvitalism in the early Greeks cf. Karl Joel, *Der
Ursprung der Naturphilosophie aus dem Geiste der Mystik*, Jena, 1926.
He discusses the pre-Socratics in relation to German romanticists, esp.
Novalis and Schelling. An impressive number of scholars support Hennig
Brinkmann's notion that life is the central idea of romanticism (*Die Idee
des Lebens in der deutschen Romantik*, Augsburg-Köln, Filser, 1926, p. 11),
notably, H. A. Korff (*Die Lebensidee Goethes*, Leipzig, Weber, 1925). Paul
Kluckhohn says that romantic philosophy in general is *Lebensphilosophie*
(*Das Ideengut der deutschen Romantik*, Tübingen, Niemeyer, 1953, p. 31).
Herbert Cysarz says "The idea of life is the cradle of all categories"
(*Erfahrung und Idee*, Vienna and Leipzig, Braumüller, 1921, p. 159). Gode
von Aesch: "Romantic thought is biocentric thought" (*Natural Science in
German Romanticism*, New York, Col. Univ. Press, 1941, p. 13). Of great
significance are several of Kroner's remarks on Hegel, e.g., "Hegel was a
Romanticist in his longing for unity . . . he called this basic unity 'life'—

munal breath of nature." [3] Wordsworth speaks of the "one
interior life That lives in all things," and of "an active
principle alive In all things, in all natures." [4] Life is an
essential attribute of reality itself; the sense of life is the
"sentiment of being:"

> I felt the sentiment of Being spread
> O'er all that moves, and all that seemeth still,
> O'er all, that, lost beyond the reach of thought
> And human knowledge, to the human eye
> Invisible, yet liveth to the heart,
> O'er all that leaps, and runs, and shouts, and sings,
> Or beats the gladsome air, o'er all that glides
> Beneath the wave, yea, in the wave itself
> And mighty depth of waters. Wonder not
> If such my transports were; for in all things now
> I saw one life.[5]

Being *is* life. "Life is the essential element of all things;
the accidental element is merely the kind of life things
have, and even that which is dead in nature is not in itself
dead; it is only extinguished life." [6]

Wordsworth senses two kinds of life, a life of stillness
and calm and a life of motion and activity: the moment
of fulfillment and that of striving. In calmness he senses "a
life that breathes not." [7] But even this "extinguished life"
is a form of activity in the same way that fulfillment is a

a term which retained some of its original spell over him even after it had
been superseded by the word 'Geist' " (*Early Theological Writings*, trans.
T. M. Knox, Chicago, Univ. of Chicago Press, 1948, p. 15). The importance
of "life" for Hegel is also pointed out by Dilthey (*Gesammelte Schriften*,
4, 59 ff., 137 ff.).

3. 2, 503.
4. Fragment in *The Prelude*, p. 512; fragment in *5*, 286, composed
1797-98.
5. *The Prelude*, II, 420-30.
6. Schelling, 2, 500.
7. "Address to Kilchurn Castle, Upon Loch Awe," l. 6.

form of striving; activity is the fundamental quality. "Absolute calm in the world is a non-thing; all calm in the world is only seeming." [8] Life is everywhere "the pulse of Being." [9] Wordsworth's deepest calm is an active calm, a seeming calm; it is "merely silent nature's breathing life." [1] Even in speaking of the life that breathes not, Wordsworth uses "breathing" in the description. Silent nature always has this pulsing overtone; the description includes terms of nonextinguished life, terms of motion and activity. The stillness is like the temporary, pulsing sleep of striving, like a moment of fusion with the living source of things:

> Dear God! the very houses seem asleep.

> the calm
> That Nature breathes among the hills and groves.

> There is a stillness, and they seem to make
> Calm revelry in that their calm abode.

> The leaves stir not,
> They all are steady as the cloudless sky;
> How deep the Quiet: all is motionless,
> As if the life of the vast world was hushed
> Into a breathless dream.[2]

At other times everything springs into joyous motion. The pulse of being is seen directly in the activity of things:

> Witness the delight
> With which erewhile I saw that multitude
> Wheel through the sky, and see them now at rest,
> Yet not at rest, upon the glassy lake.

8. Schelling, 2, 383.
9. *The Prelude*, VIII, 626.
1. "Elegiac Stanzas" (Peele Castle), l. 28.
2. "Sonnet Composed upon Westminster Bridge," l. 13; *The Prelude*, I, 284–5; *The Recluse*, ll. 586–7, 5, 333; fragment, 5, 343.

They *cannot* rest, they gambol like young whelps;
Active as lambs, and overcome with joy,
They try all frolic motions; flutter, plunge,
And beat the passive water with their wings.[3]

Lamb once said that in Wordsworth's poetry "nothing in
Nature is dead," and he added, "Motion is synonymous
with life." [4] Wordsworth's recurring sense of universal activity makes

The surface of the universal earth
With triumph, and delight, and hope, and fear,
Work like a sea.[5]

These observations lead to a tentative, preliminary definition: Life is activity. All things are, in some sense, alive
because they are in some sense active.

A second aspect of Enthusiasm's panvitalism is suggested
by Coleridge's phrase, "Each thing has a life of its own, and
we are all one life." [6] Life reflects the pattern of fusion in
separation. The separateness of individual things is preserved, and yet all things belong to "the Life Of the great
whole." [7] Life is autonomous activity and, at the same
time, reciprocal activity. Life expresses the experience of
simultaneous separation and kinship.

Each thing has a life of its own. Like world, which is
self-sufficient and self-productive, so is thing in itself and
by itself active. That is the meaning of its individuality
and life. "Life," says Schelling, "is autonomy in appearance." Going further, he asserts, "No part of nature can

3. *The Recluse*, ll. 544–51, 5, 331–2.
4. In his article on *The Excursion* in *The Quarterly Review*, October,
1814, pp. 102–3.
5. *The Prelude*, I, 499–501.
6. Cf. The letter to Sotheby, September 10, 1802, in *Collected Letters of
Samuel Taylor Coleridge*, ed. E. L. Griggs (2 vols., London, Oxford Univ.
Press, 1956), 2, 864.
7. *The Prelude*, III, 130–1.

be mere being, merely an affirmed thing. Rather, every thing is, in itself, just as much self-affirmation as conscious-ness or ego is. It follows that each thing, conceived in its true essence, can be considered with equal validity both a mode of being [affirmed being] and a mode of self-knowl-edge [affirming being]. That something exists means that it asserts itself, activates itself." [8] And for Wordsworth, life is associated with the inner principle of autonomous ac-tivity. "Independent" and "living" seem interchangeable epithets:

> supreme must be the power
> Of living Nature.
>> the enduring majesty and power
> Of independent nature.

There are places

>> That hold by an inalienable right
>> An independent Life.[9]

The pulse of being is a self-productive, active "under-presence" in rocks and stones and trees. We see into the life of things when we sense the underlying, independent self-activity of things:

>> The river glideth at his own sweet will.[1]

In observing a running hare, Wordsworth also sees the independent activity of the mist raised from the "plashy earth."

> The grass is bright with rain-drops;—on the moors
> The hare is running races in her mirth;
> And with her feet she from the plashy earth
> Raises a mist; that, glittering in the sun,
> Runs with her all the way, wherever she doth run.[2]

8. *1*, 249; 7, 53.
9. *The Prelude*, V, 166–7; VIII, 784–5. Fragment, 2, 479–80.
1. "Sonnet Composed upon Westminster Bridge," l. 12.
2. "Resolution and Independence," ll. 10–14.

Of course, the hare *causes* the mist, but here the feature of causality is underplayed. Causality is an external principle; it directs attention away from the internal principle of life. There seems to be a mutual fitting together of hare and mist like the reciprocal relation of mind and world. The activity of each element seems separate, self-activity, and yet both activities are fitted to each other. The relation of hare to mist seems an *organic* relation, one in which each of the two elements is joined to the other while each retains an active autonomy. Kant held that the organic must be considered as if it were simultaneously cause and effect of itself, and that is true both of the organization as a whole and of each part. The part is self-sustaining and self-activating, but only within the organic whole. The whole system of relationships is, as it were, the ground and context of the individual activity of the parts. "We cannot do better," says Schelling, "than to assert that neither of the two opposing processes determines the other, but that they both reciprocally determine themselves; both reciprocally hold the equilibrium." [3] Life is autonomous activity, but both activity and autonomy have their being within the context of reciprocal relationships. God is in things and, therefore, each thing is autonomous, holy, and self-active. But God is also through things, binding their self-activities in harmonious, reciprocal relationships. Life is the terrestrial, the "natural" expression for God. God is the life of each thing and also "the one Presence, and the Life Of the great whole." [4] Divine life makes all things equal in holy worth,[5] and it unites all things; it is the "living copula." [6] It guarantees individuality *and* unity, sep-

3. 2, 549.

4. *The Prelude*, III, 130–1.

5. Cf. G. Harper, *William Wordsworth* (3d ed. New York, Scribners, 1929), pp. 524–5: "Even the great doctrine of the 'life' of what men call 'inanimate' objects is a part of the leveling process favored by the Revolution."

6. 2, 374: "die lebendige Copula."

aration *and* kinship. World is the divine organism. "In every organism there must rule the highest unity of the life process from the standpoint of the whole, and, at the same time, there must rule the highest individuality of the life process from the point of view of the individual organ. But both of these cannot be combined unless one assumes that there is one and the same life process [God] in every individual being which infinitely individuates itself." God, the divine life, is the "One in All, recognizable in every part of matter; all lives only in Him. But just as directly present and recognizable in every part is the All in One, as it everywhere discloses life." [7] Each thing is

> Itself a living part of a live whole,
> A creek of the vast sea.

And it is God who is

> the life
> Of all things and the mighty unity
> In all which we behold, and feel, and are.[8]

Characteristically, both Schelling and Wordsworth look from the standpoint of the whole: "There is one Fate for all things, one Life, one Death. . . . There is but one world." [9]

> Thou art to me but as a wave
> Of the wild sea.[1]

The life of individual things is ineradicable, but there is a constant emphasis on the mighty unity, on the purposive, harmonious interactions of things which constitute the life of the great whole. Given separation and individuality,

7. Schelling, 2, 520, 377.
8. *The Prelude*, III, 625–6; XIII, 253–5.
9. Schelling, 4, 314.
1. "To a Highland Girl," ll. 55–6.

isolation is exorcised by constant reference to essential unity, to the rational, purposive, harmonious process which is the whole:

> all else
> Meets foes irreconcilable, and at best
> Doth live but by variety of disease.[2]

Isolation, disconnection, unbalance are varieties of disease. The harmony of the constant interactions amongst things is comparable to the health of an organism. But harmony is guaranteed because the world is a divine life. The very essence of things reflects activity, reciprocality. That is what Schelling means when he says that organism is the ground of mechanism, and not vice versa.[3] The harmony of things is explicable not through a mechanistic, causal pattern, but through the inner organizing principle of life. "With an eye made quiet by the power of harmony," says Wordsworth, "we see into the life of things."

The same emphasis on the divine life of the whole provides a sense of immortality. The individual life is immortal because it is part of and an expression of the harmonious living whole. The great unity "constantly guides all things in an eternal circulation," which is the immortal life of the whole. "In the coming and going of things the All contemplates his own holy and infinite life." "Thus everything, in so far as it is in God, is itself absolute, beyond all time and has an eternal life." [4] Only isolation from "the ever-living Universe" [5] means death. So long as we remain part of the immortal whole, we cannot die. Looking at his "immortal" vale, Wordsworth's young recluse says,

2. *The Prelude*, X, 174–6.
3. Cf. especially the introduction to *Ideen zu einer Philosophie der Natur*, 2, 1–73.
4. Schelling, 2, 374; 7, 168; 4, 250.
5. *The Prelude*, VI, 701.

> "What happy fortune were it here to live!
> And, if a thought of dying, if a thought
> Of *mortal separation,* could intrude
> With paradise before him, here to die!" [6]

The "feeling of life endless" comes upon us when we truly participate in the "ennobling Harmony" which constitutes the divine life of nature.

> The Spirit of Nature was upon me here;
> The Soul of Beauty and enduring life
> Was present as a habit, and diffused,
> Through meagre lines and colours, and the press
> Of self-destroying, transitory things
> Composure and ennobling Harmony. [7]

In another passage, Wordsworth makes explicit the connection between the immortality of things and the great circulation, the "revolving life," expressed by the infinite ebbing and flowing of things:

> he had early learned
> To reverence the volume which displays
> The mystery, the life which cannot die;
> But in the mountains did he *feel* his faith
> There did he see the writing—All things there
> Looked immortality, revolving life,
> And greatness still revolving, infinite;
> There littleness was not, the least of things
> Seemed infinite. [8]

We are immortal because we are, as Schelling said, "in God" and part of His eternal life. Death is only another sort of participation, just as calmness is another sort of activity. Death is only "extinguished life," a return to the

---

6. *The Recluse,* ll. 11–14, 5, 313. Italics mine.
7. *The Prelude,* XIII, 183; VII, 735–40.
8. *The Ruined Cottage,* ll. 146–54, 5, 382–3.

dormant source of nature's silent circulation. Wordsworth, thinking once of his own possible early death, imagined that

> A poor mistaken and bewilder'd offering,
> Should to the breast of Nature have gone back.[9]

And nowhere is the return to calm and silent participation in the great circulation better expressed than in the famous lines,

> No motion has she now, no force;
> She neither hears nor sees;
> Rolled round in earth's diurnal course,
> With rocks, and stones, and trees.[1]

But the God through things is also the God in things. Activating the harmonious totality is the divine presence subsisting at the innermost core of every part. Both notions are true: a thing is alive insofar as it participates in the living whole, and a thing participates in the living whole insofar as it is alive. The idea of causality is again inapplicable. Immortality is an attribute of individual things as well as of the whole. The one life is also many lives.[2] God is present in each part. Things become self-destroying and transitory when they become in some way disconnected or isolated. God becomes cut off from Himself. But life never can be charmed or stilled. It is "A Presence which is not to be put by."

A thought is with me sometimes, and I say,
Should earth by inward throes be wrench'd throughout,

---

9. *The Prelude*, X, 197–8.

1. "A Slumber did my Spirit Seal," ll. 5–8.

2. Cf. M. M. Rader, *Presiding Ideas in Wordsworth's Poetry* (Seattle, U. of Washington Press, 1931), p. 174: "Such examples show that there is no sharp cleavage between passages in which the poet definitely attributes 'souls' or 'presences' to nature, and passages in which he achieves a pervasive atmosphere that seems to express a totality of life."

Or fire be sent from far to wither all
Her pleasant habitations, and dry up
Old Ocean in his bed left sing'd and bare,
Yet would the living Presence still subsist
Victorious; and composure would ensue,
And kindlings like the morning.[3]

Oetinger's discipline (see the epigraph to this chapter)
for seeing the universal life of things concerns the self as
well as God. Enthusiasm never submerges the self. The
experience of subject-object separation is just as ineradicable as the sense of subject-object kinship. The activity
of striving is a reciprocal activity between subject and object, yet it is also an indispensable element within ego itself. Ego is itself active, but this activity is not cut off from
nonego or otherness any more than God is cut off from
Himself. Ego is not static, but constantly involved in a
reciprocal relation with otherness. Because of this continuous reciprocal activity, selfhood is neither submerged nor
cut off and isolated. For Enthusiasm, life is the essence of
selfhood. Life, like Divinity, is self-sustaining, self-gener-
ating activity, and, at the same time, reciprocal activity.
Enthusiasm's emphasis upon life is an affirmation of selfhood as such. When the Hindu discipline aims at a complete submersion of self in a larger, total self, it automatically aims at the death of the individual self as an
ontological reality. Enthusiasm, viewing *life* as the essence
of both self and nonself, gives the individual ego an in-
violable ontological status. For life implies autonomy.
From the inner, rather than the cosmic, external point of
view, life and selfhood are interchangeable terms. The
emphasis upon life is an assertion of the ineradicable selfhood of things as individuals.

At the same time, the vital selfhood of each thing

3. *The Prelude,* V, 28-35.

parallels the selfhood of every other thing. Life expresses the kinship of all things. "He who begins in himself to know himself and holds up to his own nature other animated things will at length discern in animals, plants, and stones a single uniform life." The penetration of a thing's selfhood is an intuition of its life. A dead object, says Schelling, "is a selfless object." "As long as I am identical with nature, I understand what a living nature is as well as I understand my own life. . . . But as soon as I separate myself (and with me everything ideal) from nature, there is nothing left for me but a dead object, and I cease to comprehend how it is that life outside of me is possible." [4] Life is the bond of self and other, the source of

> those first-born affinities that fit
> Our new existence to existing things.[5]

Life is "the secret bond which connects our spirit with nature." It is the "visible analogy of mental being." [6]

Universal life thus means universal selfhood. The sensing of selfhood in the object is nothing less than a feeling of kinship with the object, a *feeling with,* an emotional identification.

> To every natural form, rock, fruit or flower,
> Even the loose stones that cover the high-way,
> I gave a moral life, I saw them feel,
> Or link'd them to some feeling.[7]

The attribution of feeling to things accompanies the attribution of life and selfhood to them. Universal life or

---

4. *1*, 358; *2*, 47–8.

5. *The Prelude*, I, 582–3.

6. *2*, 55: "Was ist denn jenes geheime Band, das unsern Geist mit der Natur verknüpft?" The context makes it clear that the answer is "Das Leben"; *1*, 388: "Denn nur das Leben ist das sichtbare Analogon des geistigen Seyns."

7. *The Prelude*, III, 124–7.

selfhood is the source of those "silent, unobtrusive sympathies" between man and nature.[8] Wordsworth speaks of the "love that comes wherever life and sense Are given by God,"[9] and Schelling discusses "the attraction of inner love and sympathy between thine own spirit and living nature." He describes the ubiquitous feeling-with in nature, and he views this as an expression of the universality and continuity of life: "The sadness and even wailing of many an animal, together with a changed color in the sky, has forecast the outbreak of great earthquakes, as if the same cause which shakes mountains and raises islands out of the sea also heaves the breathing breast of animals.—Experiences which one cannot explain without assuming a general continuity in all natural things and a common medium through which alone all forces of nature exercise an effect upon the sensible being. This principle sustains the continuity of the inorganic and organic world and binds the whole of nature into a general organism."[1] Universal life implies universal love, the self-sympathetic life of God in and through things.

The kind of love that interests Wordsworth and Schelling is not, therefore, the variety which selects one particular self as its "object."

> Thy love is human merely; this proceeds
> More from the brooding Soul, and is divine.[2]

It is a general, diffuse love which springs from the self's emotional identification with the cosmos.

> Thou art to me but as a wave
> Of the wild sea.

It is

8. Ibid., II, 316.
9. "To a Dog," ll. 27-8, *4, 79*.
1. 7, 62; 2, 569.
2. *The Prelude*, XIII, 164-5.

the pure joy of love,
By sound diffus'd, or by the breathing air,
Or by the silent looks of happy things,
Or flowing from the universal face
Of earth and sky.[3]

It is the "miracle of *essential* love, which strives through opposition to unite with itself." [4]

The feeling of cosmic sympathy is a correlate to Enthusiasm's sense of cosmic life. The two are interdependent. Cosmic sympathy is kinship in separation, fulfillment in striving. It defines the structure of experience when the category of experience is (and it is always) life. Scheler's comments in *The Nature of Sympathy* are illuminating:

> Identification with the cosmos cannot really take place except within a view of things which envisages the world as a whole, a *collective organism,* permeated by a *unitary* life; it requires an organic mode of approach to things. Given such a viewpoint, the ideal and real (teleological or causal) connections between things, as studied in science and philosophy, are supplemented by a new sort of relationship, co-extensive with what is real in life generally. It is that which holds between life and its *mode of expression,* a specifically symbolic relation. It is intrinsically impossible to identify with the inanimate, when presented as such (and fellow-feeling is plainly ruled out as well: this latter point, indeed, being much more obvious than the other). Identification can extend to the cosmos only if those Ideas and Forms of Intuition which have pure and immediate application to the organic element in experience, are super-

3. *The Ruined Cottage*, ll. 98–102, 5, 408.
4. Schelling, 7, 59.

imposed also on dead matter, its changes and motions, doings and undergoings, its coming-to-be and passing-away. Only then do *all* natural phenomena appear both as the undivided total life of a single world-organism and the universal fluid matrix in which it is expressed.[5]

Enthusiasm's cosmic sympathy is expressed as love of *nature*. Nature is a category which is, to a large extent, inherited. But nature is not simply a historical given. Enthusiasm appropriated that which was meaningful for itself, and it modified what it appropriated to conform with the general structure of its attitudes. Enthusiasm took from the Enlightenment the idea of nature's independent perfection and availability. It accepted the confident idea that nature's perfection and order is directly understandable by human reason.[6] But it modified the previous idea of nature to its own use.

It is easy to lapse into a futile scepticism about the possibility of describing what nature means for Enthusiasm. Lovejoy's investigations tend to foster such scepticism by showing that nature has been, historically, all things to all men.[7] One could well despair of pinning down a meaning which has a general or typical validity in Enthusiasm. But two considerations work against this sceptical conclusion. The first is circumstantial: nature is a single word and, regardless of its range, it must have meant something in the period when it was most often used, something which was communicated and communicable by a single word. The

5. Max Scheler, *The Nature of Sympathy*, trans. Peter Heath (London, Routledge & Kegan Paul, 1954), pp. 81–2. Cf. The later paragraphs in my discussion of "Imagination."

6. Cf. Ernst Cassirer, *The Philosophy of the Enlightenment*, trans. F. C. A. Koelln and J. P. Pettegrove (Princeton, Princeton Univ. Press, 1951), p. 39.

7. Cf. A. O. Lovejoy, "Nature as Aesthetic Norm" in *Essays in the History of Ideas*, Baltimore, Johns Hopkins Univ. Press, 1948.

second consideration goes closer to the heart of the matter. It is inevitable that nature should have meant so much. The proper conclusion is not that it meant so much as to mean nothing in particular. A more accurate way of putting the matter would be to say that nature meant indeed everything, but that it meant everything from a particular viewpoint which provided a particular set of emphases.[8] Nature is not limited to a particular segment of reality; it is the whole of reality viewed as having a particular sort of structure and value.

It is useful to provide a preliminary (and temporary) definition. The central aspect of nature is nonhuman external reality, the world of animals, plants, and stones, "the operations of the elements, and the appearances of the visible universe," those things which come and go, as well as those things which are "great and permanent." [9] Let us call this nonhuman external reality Prime Nature. Enthusiasm focuses upon Prime Nature as providing a sanction for its view of the totality. Such a focus implies an emphasis upon the here and now, on that which is everywhere immediately available. For the here and now is the locus of value. Such a focus emphasizes also the omnipresent functioning of discernible and immutable laws.

Prime Nature is beautifully lawful. It exhibits a perfect, teleological order; it exemplifies design. Wordsworth calls attention to inevitable teleology when he speaks of

8. Cf. Schelling, 5, 317: "Wenn wir von der Natur absolut reden wollen, so verstehen wir darunter das Universum ohne Gegensatz."

9. Wordsworth, preface (1800), 2, 397. Lovejoy corroborates: "The word 'nature' had long since come to designate, along with its many other meanings, the whole world of sensible objects and its ordinary processes and empirically known laws" ("Nature as Norm in Tertullian," *Essays*, p. 324). As I point out in the chapter on "Imagination," Prime Nature is most accurately equatable to "unconscious" nature, whether human or nonhuman.

"the tide of things," and of "the calm oblivious tendencies of nature." [1] Schelling is more specific; the basic *law* of nature is the interaction of two forces:

> In nature everything strives continually forward. Since this is the case, we must seek the reason in a principle which, being an inexhaustible source of positive force, begins the movement ever anew and unceasingly sustains it. This positive principle is the first force of Nature. But an invisible power guides all appearances in the world back to the eternal circulation. Since this is the case, we must seek the reason in a negative force, which constantly limits the effects of the positive principle, which constantly guides the general movement back to its source. This negative principle is the second force of Nature. [2]

But there is a fundamental difference between Enthusiasm's conception of nature's immutable order and that of the Enlightenment. Schelling may use terms like "positive force" and "negative force," but his notion of law in nature has little to do with the concept of patterned causality. For the Enlightenment, nature's order and coherence was *explained* by laws which were, presumably, put into effect by a divine Lawmaker. But Enthusiasm does not explain in a causal fashion. Even when speaking of "forces," Schelling is not describing a causal pattern. His ground category is not causality, but reciprocality. [3] He never forgets that nature is the "essence of God carried over into form." [4] Patterned causality is the outside of

---

1. "The Old Cumberland Beggar," l. 164; *The Ruined Cottage*, l. 114.

2. 2, 381. These forces are given elsewhere the names "light" and "gravity." Note that they are employed to describe a process which moves in a circle. The emphasis is not on a causal pattern but on the *inter*action of forces which produces a living form. Life moves, grows (positive principle), but returns to its source (negative principle).

3. Cf. 3, 469–78. On p. 475, e.g., we find: "Es ist überhaupt kein Causalitätsverhältniss construirbar ohne Wechselwirkung."

4. 2, 66.

things, which shows that the divine hand is above all, controlling all. But divinity is also within things; it is an internal "Presence" which guarantees the reciprocity of things. What is law from the outside is, from the inside, life.

> The laws of things which lie
> Beyond the reach of human will or power;
> The life of nature, by the God of love
> Inspired, celestial presence ever pure.[5]

The external, Newtonian "forces" interact reciprocally in a great self-sustaining harmony because the internal "law" of things is life. It is a God of love who inspires the life of nature, for love expresses the reciprocal internality of separate things, just as universal life expresses universal internality. And Enthusiasm senses this selfhood in Prime Nature as being akin to man's own selfhood. It senses what Wordsworth calls an "underpresence" and what Schelling calls *Ichheit*.[6] It is this underpresence which evokes Wordsworth's

> sympathy
> With nature in her forms inanimate,
> With objects such as have no power to hold
> Articulate language. In all forms of things
> There is a mind.[7]

That is the sense in which Prime Nature has a "soul." Along with their outward harmony, things have an underpresence of selfhood and divinity which is life.

> O! Soul of Nature! that dost overflow
> With passion and with life.[8]

5. *The Prelude*, XI, 97–100.
6. Cf. *The Prelude*, p. 513, and my remarks on love toward the end of Ch. 6.
7. MS fragment, 5, 340.
8. *The Prelude*, XI, 146–7.

The law which Prime Nature exhibits in the order and harmony of its processes is, then, the law of life. More specifically, it is the law of organization. "Organism is the principle of things." [9] The organism is the model for all reality, the *Urbild* which Prime Nature everywhere exemplifies.[1] In focusing attention upon Prime Nature, Enthusiasm intuits the quality of *all* reality. "From the moss which has scarcely a visible trace of organization up to the noblest form which seems to have brushed aside the fetters of matter, there is one and the same force, which working according to one and the same ideal of harmonious interaction, strives to express . . . into infinity one and the same *Urbild*." This Urbild of organization is the underpresence of all natural things. "This one in all is recognizable in every part of matter, all lives only in God. But just as directly present and recognizable in every part is the all in one, as it everywhere discloses life." [2] It is this revelation which the things in Prime Nature provide.

> But though the picture weary out the eye,
> By nature an unmanageable sight,
> It is not wholly so to him who looks
> In steadiness, who hath among least things

9. 2, 500: "Der Organismus ist nicht die Eigenschaft einzelner Naturdinge, sondern umgekehrt, die einzelnen Naturdinge sind ebenso viele Beschränkungen oder einzelne Anschauungsweisen des allgemeinen Organismus. . . . Die Dinge sind also nicht Principien des Organismus, sondern umgekehrt, der Organismus ist das Principium der Dinge."

1. A simple way of conceiving this: In an organism, intermediate organs are themselves organisms, and this is, further, true of individual cells within the organs. Each part preserves a degree of autonomy because elements within it interact to sustain it, just as the organs interact to sustain the organism as a whole. There is both autonomy and reciprocal activity (interdependence) at every level. Cf. Schelling, *1*, 387: "Jede Organisation ist eine vereinigte Welt. . . . Es ist ein ewiges Urbild, das in jeder Pflanze ausgedrückt ist."

2. Schelling, *1*, 387; *2*, 377.

An under-sense of greatest; sees the parts
As parts, but with a feeling of the whole.[3]

Those lines express something fundamental in the enthusiastic way of viewing things. Least things both participate in and typify the great organic whole. Enthusiasm
exhibits everywhere the tendency to intuit the whole in
the part. It is not content to remain with the individual
part simply as such. The individual parts are valuable
because they are not merely individual parts; they express
the whole, they are Urbilder of the infinite totality.

What want we? have we not perpetual streams,
Warm woods, and sunny hills, and fresh green fields,
And mountains not less green, and flocks, and herds,
And thickets full of songsters, and the voice
Of lordly birds, an unexpected sound
Heard now and then from morn to latest eve,
Admonishing the man who walks below
Of solitude, and silence in the sky?
These have we, and a thousand nooks of earth
Have also these.[4]

It is not only these things but also the universality of these
things which Enthusiasm beholds. And that universality
is assured by the inner kinship of all things. "Just as the
ground of all activity in Nature is one, omnipresent, conditioned by nothing else, and is absolute in relation to
each thing, so the different activities are distinguished
from one another only in form. But none of these forms is
dependent on another; each is, in its own way, the same
as the other." [5]

3. *The Prelude*, VII, 707–12. Wordsworth is speaking of London rather
than of Prime Nature, but the principle is in every case the same.
4. *The Recluse*, ll. 126–35, 5, 317.
5. Schelling, 5, 320. This is, I think, the most important source of the
symbolizing tendency in romantic poetry. The symbolic image both par-

Another way of expressing the part-whole relationship in Enthusiasm's mode of perception is to say that the species is intuited in the individual. The individual is sensed as playing a divine role in the scheme of things; it tends to merge with the species, just as the species tends to represent (as Urbild) the whole in a particular stage or moment. The individual is a moment in the species just as the species is a moment in "the mighty commonwealth of things."

> Happy is he who lives to understand,
> Observes, explores, for this that he may find
> The law, and what it is, and where begins
> The union and disunion, that which makes
> Degree or kind in every shape of being,
> The constitutions, powers, and faculties,
> And habits and enjoyments that assign
> To every class its office or abode
> Through all the mighty commonwealth of things.[6]

The individual *becomes* the species. Here and now, the individual expresses for the species what Prime Nature expresses for the whole of reality. In the *present* particular experience the glory of the whole is felt. The edges are dimmed, the individual stretches out into long vistas of infinity, value lies at hand before us. For the present experience "is not simply the product of an incomprehensible creating but this creating itself; not only the appearance or revelation of the eternal, rather, at the same time, precisely this eternal itself." [7]

---

ticipates in and represents the whole. Romantic symbols tend to be synechdoches not for rhetorical so much as for metaphysical reasons.

6. MS verses associated with *The Excursion*, ll. 332–42 (written in 1800). Cf. Wordsworth, 5, 119.

7. Schelling, 2, 378.

Schelling's identification of the created thing with the principle of creativity calls attention to another dimension. Just as the individual participates in and represents the species, so does the created thing participate in and represent the divine, creative source of things. In the present experience one apprehends the source whence the experience proceeds. The very quality of that experience gives assurance that all things come from God as plant from seed. Especially, the inner kinship of the appearances in Prime Nature provides hints that the vast organism proceeds from a divine seed. "The inner type of all things must be one because of the common source." [8] The common underpresence is a vestige of the pantheistic moment:

> The outward shows of sky and earth,
> Of hill and valley, he has viewed;
> And impulses of deeper birth
> Have come to him in solitude.[9]

The deeper birth of those impulses is found not only in the poet but also in the outward shows. Both have a common internality because both have a common divine source. This source is "the unity out of which everything in Nature goes forth," "the common ground from which everything flows." And it is also the unity to which everything returns, for nature is "the eternal birth of God in things, and the likewise eternal gathering again of things into God." [1] The appearances of Prime Nature never depart from the path of this great circulation. Prime Nature is never far from the divine source. That is the profound meaning of its immutable orderly processes. For this reason, love of nature is, as Wordsworth describes it,

8. Schelling, 5, 325.
9. "A Poet's Epitaph," ll. 45–8.
1. Schelling, 5, 327, 320; 7, 59.

> service but to things which lie
> At rest, within the bosom of thy will.[2]

Thus, Prime Nature can never "betray Or disappoint her genuine Votary." [3] For we find there divine harmony, perfect obedience in the bosom of God's will. And the closeness to God of Prime Nature is seen also in those aspects of humanity which are, like Prime Nature, unconscious, instinctive expressions of life. Such aspects are found in children:

> Dear Child! dear Girl! that walkest with me here,
> If thou appear untouched by solemn thought,
> Thy nature is not therefore less divine:
> Thou liest in Abraham's bosom all the year;
> And worshipp'st at the Temple's inner shrine,
> God being with thee when we know it not.[4]

But human identity with Prime Nature is not limited to children. The identity is expressed by human thinghood in general. Like man, Prime Nature has a soul, a universal internality which is an expression of its universal life; at the same time, human beings are things, like the unconscious things in Prime Nature:

> She seemed a thing that could not feel
> The touch of earthly years.[5]

Human thinghood expresses man's identity with Prime Nature and, therefore, man's ultimate lodgment in the bosom of God's will. Found especially, but not exclusively, in the instinctive, almost inarticulate life of children and

2. *The Prelude*, X, 396–7. Cf. also "Nature's self which is the breath of God," ibid., V, 222.

3. MS fragment, Wordsworth, 5, 477.

4. "It is a beauteous evening," ll. 9–14.

5. "A slumber did my spirit seal," ll. 3–4.

country folk, human thinghood means identification with Prime Nature and closeness to God.

> And her's shall be the breathing balm,
> And her's the silence and the calm
> Of mute insensate things.[6]

Such identification of conscious humanity with the unconscious processes of Prime Nature is possible (see Chapter 6) because there is, in fact, no radical distinction made between nonconscious thinghood and conscious humanity. Both express the one divine life within us and abroad. For there is but one life, one world, one nature: "One Nature as there is one Sun in heaven." [7] And the meaning of Prime Nature, of man, of any part, is the meaning of the whole. That is the undersense of greatness which imbues everything; it is the final meaning of nature. In the divine organism in which man is privileged to participate, everything (including man) "is in every case the expression of the entire All." [8] Every part is both moment and Urbild; every individual is both individual and kind and, whatever its place in the whole, carries a divine value. Cosmic love, the love of nature, is sanctioned by the universal Urbild of life which makes the whole world kin. That is the basis for Schelling's Philosophy of Identity as well as for Wordsworth's poetry of common life. Each thing is both an unconscious agent and an active self. For the whole is one, divine, self-affirmative, and alive.

6. "Three years she grew," ll. 16–18.
7. *The Prelude*, X, 141.
8. Schelling, 5, 378.

5. Time

ENTHUSIASM DENIES the radical nature of time; there is no absolute separation between time and eternity. Just as in the case of all other oppositions, time and eternity interfuse. In fact, Enthusiasm *has* to hold this view of time in order to sustain the dynamic unity of opposites in all the other realms, for, once the inexorability of temporal flux is admitted, everything else falls into disconnection. The fusion that is striven for has to be *there* already, otherwise the moment of separation would be absolute; it would be gone, past recalling, never to be redeemed. Yet Enthusiasm has to accept movement through time, otherwise striving would have no meaning. All would be static perfection, eternal redemption. Temporality alone gives a meaning to striving and to life; nontemporality alone gives a meaning to the feeling of ever-present fulfillment and affirmation. Enthusiasm needs both time and eternity, and it needs them together.

Some of Schelling's attempts to express this difficult paradox have, as Fuhrmans points out, "a dangerous tendency toward the static, and therefore raise many problems for the *Identitätsystem*. But this stasis is the reverse of what Schelling really wants to assert." [1] Stasis

1. Fuhrmans, *Schellings Philosophie*, p. 57.

would destroy the whole meaning of striving and of life. Nevertheless, it cannot be overlooked that many of Schelling's pronouncements smack of Parmenides. Time becomes a mere derived category, derived from Being which is eternally self-identical. "Nothing, from the viewpoint of Being, arises." "There lives an unchangeable, ever self-identical Being. All activity and movement stems merely from the limited perspective of an individual." Such assertions point more to the difficulty of the problem Schelling was trying to solve than to its actual solution. The path of that solution is complex. One cannot quite agree with Schelling when he tells us, "It is only mental laziness if thou be unconscious of seeing time as eternity and eternity as time." [2]

The solution of the problem is fundamentally a religious one. If we understand Being as another word for God, then the remarks about static Being take on a new significance. Schelling says, "there lives" a Being, unchanging and self-identical. God is not static but alive. Being is life. The temporal-eternal is God's life expressed in the real. "All that has happened and all that happens is the production of the One Intelligence which has not begun and will not cease to be." For this reason, "every particular moment of time is the revelation of a particular side of God in which He is absolute." The temporal-eternal vision perceives all things as in God and part of His eternal life. The intuition of the world's temporal-eternal nature is an intuition of the divine nature and purpose (*Selbstbejahung*). "Everything insofar as it is in God is itself absolute, beyond all time and has an eternal life." [3]

Nowhere does Wordsworth express this intuition of the temporal-eternal so well as in the description of the

2. *4*, 119, 314; *7*, 63.
3. *3*, 487; *5*, 288; *4*, 250.

Simplon Pass. Journeying for several hours through the pass, the poet sees

> The immeasurable height
> Of woods decaying, never to be decay'd,
> The stationary blasts of water-falls.

These scenes of "tumult *and* peace" Wordsworth calls the "types and symbols of eternity." [4] The moving waterfall is a stationary blast—at once movement and stasis. The streaming water seems arrested even as it moves, just as a moment caught in the moving stream of time is in some way beyond time. The moment passes away and yet remains forever. This aspect of the temporal-eternal vision might be characterized as "the immortality of the present."

The heart of the experience is that value (fulfillment) is preserved in the midst of time's flux (striving). "What is true, what is right and beautiful, is, by its very nature, eternal, and in the midst of time, has no relationship to time." [5] This truth is intuited especially in those moments when the truth, beauty, and rightness of the whole world-process are grasped in a single finite experience. Such moments do not pass away; they sustain (and reflect) the meaning of the great affirmation which characterizes both the world-process and the stream of experience itself. Visually, in nature, such moments are the "types and symbols of eternity," which is to say that they at once symbolize and participate in the divine process. From the viewpoint of experience, such moments become

> spots of time,
> Which with distinct pre-eminence retain
> A vivifying Virtue.[6]

4. *The Prelude*, VI, 556–72. Italics mine.
5. Schelling, 5, 224.
6. *The Prelude*, XI, 258–60.

Just before the passage about woods and waterfalls, Wordsworth provides an apostrophe to that faculty which permits him to see types and symbols of the eternal process in the midst of his sensory experience. He calls it a power which

> In all the might of its endowments, came
> Athwart me; I was lost as in a cloud,
> Halted, without a struggle to break through.
> And now recovering, to my Soul I say
> I recognise thy glory; in such strength
> Of usurpation, in such visitings
> Of awful promise, when the light of sense
> Goes out in flashes that have shewn to us
> The invisible world, doth Greatness make abode,
> There harbours whether we be young or old.

In the midst of sensory experience, the mind transcends sensory flux and intuits the "invisible world" which comprehends the eternal wholeness and unity toward which we strive. In the spots-of-time passage, there is a similar emphasis on the faculty's nonsensuous quality. The light of sense must go out; the mind must control objective experience rather than be controlled by it.

> This efficacious spirit chiefly lurks
> Among those passages of life in which
> We have had deepest feeling that the mind
> Is lord and master, and that outward sense
> Is but the obedient servant of her will.[7]

Finite temporality, it would seem, is supplied by objects— by the succession of sensory perceptions which they *impose* upon our minds. In special moments, however, the mind would seem to impose upon these passing images (perhaps

7. Ibid. VI, 528–37; XI, 269–73.

by obliterating them) the sense of an eternal realm in which succession is arrested. The mind is able to imbue the passing images with what Wordsworth called "the indomitableness of the spirit within me." [8] The faculty or power alluded to would seem to be analogous to the "One Intelligence which has not begun and will not cease to be." It allows us for a moment to know things from the divine perspective.

In similar fashion, Schelling adduces a special faculty with like qualities. He opposes what he calls "intellectual perception" to sense perception.

> In all of us there dwells a secret, wonderful faculty which draws us away from the changes of time, from all that comes from the outside, and back to our innermost, unclothed selves. There, under the form of unchangeableness, we perceive in ourselves the eternal. . . . This faculty differs from sense perception in that it is only brought forth in freedom; it remains foreign and unknown to everyone in whom freedom is overpowered by the might of objects.

As we know, "intelligence strives in every moment to represent the absolute synthesis," [9] but only when the mind is freed from the overpowering might of objects (that is to say, from the irresistible flow of sense perceptions) can the mind really intuit the synthesis of time and eternity which God at every "moment" produces. For both Wordsworth and Schelling, the mind of man has the divine power to perceive the immortality of the moments which are seemingly caught in a finite flux. This faculty seems to come into play at special moments in man's experience.

But this psychological explanation describes only one

8. Cf. the Fenwick note on the Immortality Ode in Wordsworth, *4*, 463.

9. *1*, 318; *3*, 487.

aspect of the matter. By itself, it is inherently unsatis-factory. If the insight into present immortality requires a special, occasional faculty which is unconditioned by the objects of sense experience, then man's intercourse with the world becomes disvalued. The realm of time and of sensory experience would become a kind of illusion. This static "abyss of idealism" is the reverse of what Schelling and Wordsworth desire.[1] If the psychological explanation were the complete one, it would belie Enthusiasm's basic experience which affirms the goodness of the living reality itself. *That* is the true reality, the medium in which we are fulfilled, the matrix of all value. The moment when the light of sense goes out, when everything is seen under the aspect of eternity, is like the mystical moment when we intuit

> . the one
> Surpassing Life, which out of space and time,
> Nor touched by welterings of passion, is
> And hath the name of God.[2]

The moment of intellectual perception is a static point of fulfillment occurring within the active process of experience as a whole. It is a moment which is taken up within the process of which it forms a part. It is a moment of mystic fusion which gives direction and meaning to the larger process.

The larger process is always characterized by dynamic reciprocality. The special faculty of intellectual perception, "rising like an unfather'd vapour" and showing that "the mind is lord and master," is just as one-sided as the pure sense perception which is overpowered by the might of objects. In the larger process neither side is lord and master. When Wordsworth actually describes them, the

1. Wordsworth uses the phrase in the Fenwick note cited above
2. *The Prelude*, VI, 154–7.

spots of time are not occasions when the mind turns in *complete* freedom to its naked, eternal self; they are moments, rather, when the mind intuits *in* sensual, temporal experience an eternal quality. The mind and the concrete objects of nature work together with blended might. Even when the mind seems to be lord and master, mind and nature work reciprocally upon each other. Note the "indisputable shapes" of such an experience:

> And afterwards, the wind and sleety rain
> And all the business of the elements,
> The single sheep, and the one blasted tree,
> And the bleak music of that old stone wall,
> The noise of wood and water, and the mist
> Which on the line of each of those two Roads
> Advanced in such indisputable shapes,
> All these were spectacles and sounds to which
> I often would repair and thence would drink,
> As at a fountain.[3]

The essence of both sides is temporal-eternal; the unifying mist is out there in nature as well as in the mind like an unfathered vapor. As long as mind and nature both contribute to the experience, that experience is at once in dynamic process *and* timeless. Only outside of this reciprocity can "mortal separation" intrude. Each side corrects the other when either tends to falter into radical temporality or into radical stasis. That is the gift of the mind to nature and the gift of nature to the mind. Mind has this *privatio:* it can only function temporally. "In the empirical consciousness the whole can be conceived only through a gradual synthesis of parts, in other words, through a succession of ideas." [4] Yet, over against this succession of ideas,

3. Ibid., XI, 376–85. "Indisputable shapes" is, of course, a modification of *Hamlet*, I.4.43 (noted by de Selincourt).
4. Schelling, *3*, 482.

nature provides permanent forms like mountains and rills.
Nature is "as constant as the grass upon the fields"; Wordsworth saw it as a

fulgent spectacle
Which neither changed, nor stirr'd, nor pass'd away.[5]

Yet nature could not provide this permanent spectacle *as
a whole,* were it not for the contribution of the mind. Nature has this *privatio:* in our experience of the external
world we find that many things do not, like mountains and
rills, remain; we find mutability and "the passing shews of
being." Only the mind (sustained by nature's permanent
forms) can impose the perspective which allows the perception of immortality amidst change and evident death:

> She sleeps in the calm earth and peace is here.
> I well remember that those very plumes,
> Those weeds and the high spear-grass on that wall,
> By mist and silent rain-drops silvered o'er,
> As once I passed, did to my mind convey
> So still an image of tranquillity,
> So calm and still, and looked so beautiful,
> Amid the uneasy thoughts which filled my mind,
> That what we feel of sorrow and despair
> From ruin and from change, and all the grief
> The passing shews of being leave behind
> Appeared an idle dream that could not live
> Where meditation was.[6]

The weeds and spear-grass convey something timeless to
the mind, and in turn the mind encompasses something
timeless in the external flux.

The timeless perspective which the mind contributes to
nature and which nature sustains and corroborates in the

5. *The Prelude,* VI, 705; X, 487–8.
6. *The Ruined Cottage,* 122–34, 5, 403.

mind is not described accurately or fully by the term "present immortality." That phrase directs attention to a particular moment in experience. Yet these timeless moments do pass away, even as they in a sense remain. An expression has to be found for a general view which encompasses the whole *succession* of such moments as well as their timelessness. An expression has to be found which encompasses past, present, and future "immortality" all at once, and yet which preserves the insight that there is process, striving, dynamic activity. This expression is, as I have hinted, "life." Life, the Being of God, is at once temporal and eternal. Life changes, moves, develops; yet this movement occurs as a cycle. The cycle of life is eternal. Somewhere, everywhere, the moments of the cycle are recurring; they are, have been, and will be. To grasp the temporal-eternal view of Wordsworth and Schelling as a whole, one must grasp the meaning of cyclicity and of development within a cycle. The view of time becomes quite explicitly a view of life.

Cyclicity is fundamental to life. "Life consists in circulation, in a sequence of processes which continually return to themselves." "The basic character of life consists in this, that it is a fixed, circulatory sequence which is sustained by an inner principle." The cyclicity of organic life is a type and symbol of the temporal-eternal. "Organization is succession limited in its course; it is, as it were, stiffened succession," for it is succession which passes through a cycle, movement which returns to its own beginning. "Organization is precisely succession which returns upon itself, succession represented in peace. The concept of organization does not exclude all idea of succession. Organization is simply succession which is enclosed within boundaries and represented as fixed. The expression of the organic form is peace, even though this constant reproduction of a peaceful form is only possible because of constant internal change." The organic *is* the temporal-eternal, and the temporal-eternal characterizes the processes of nature as a whole. For nature is itself a living organism. Nature is, in fact, a living organization by virtue of its cyclic movement.

> In the external world there is a constant shifting of alterations, which, however, do not lose themselves in infinity but are limited to a definite circle within which they constantly recur. This shifting of altera- tions is therefore at once finite and infinite: finite be- cause it never goes beyond a certain boundary, infinite because it constantly returns upon itself. The circu- lar line is the fundamental synthesis of finite and infinite, within which even the straight line must resolve itself. *Succession occurs only apparently in a straight line; it actually flows constantly back to itself.*[7]

This cyclic pattern is fundamental to Wordsworth, and it lies behind the structure of many poems. "Tintern Ab- bey" provides a good example. Wordsworth, characteris- tically, is speaking of a moment in experience. The poem opens with a reference to the passage of time, a reference which measures time by the cyclic pattern of the seasons.

> Five years have past; five summers, with the length
> Of five long winters.

The passage of time in the external world is measured by the "definite circle" of recurring alterations. Likewise, the passage of time in the poet's own experience is measured by cyclic recurrence. The poet repeats experiences which occurred five years ago.

>   again I hear
> These waters . . .

7. Schelling, 2, 549; 3, 496, 493, 491, 490. Italics mine.

> Once again
> Do I behold these steep and lofty cliffs . . .
>
> The day is come [mark the note of inevitability] when
>   I again repose
> Here, under this dark sycamore . . .
>
>   Once again I see
> These hedge-rows . . .

It is this very recurrence in the outer world and in his personal experience which makes the poet aware that a change in himself has occurred. The moment when the conditions of his experience are the same brings the poet an awareness of a definite, but nonetheless welcome change. He says,

> Not for this
> Faint I, nor mourn nor murmur; other gifts
> Have followed; for such loss, I would believe,
> Abundant recompense.

Somehow the change is *compensated* for. The nature of this compensation is treated in the chapters on Imagination and on the Immortality Ode. For the present discussion, the important points are that the loss is not felt to be radical (see below) and that the change occurs within a cyclical pattern. The poet has referred to the external cyclic recurrence of the seasons and to the recurrence, through the scene before him, of a visual experience in himself. The poem ends with another sort of cyclic reference. In his younger sister, the poet sees a repetition of a stage in the larger cycle of human life. She is that which he once was, and fortified by the scene which lies before them, she will become what he is now. The poet's earlier stage exists not only ideally in his memory but actually in his sister.

> in thy voice I catch
> The language of my former heart, and read
> My former pleasures in the shooting lights
> Of thy wild eyes. Oh! yet a little while
> May I behold in thee what I was once.

The moment of the poem is, then, a moment within a living cyclical pattern, and it is at the same time an occasion for intuiting the cycle itself as a *constant* pattern.

Such emphasis on cyclicity is central to Wordsworth. For him things "looked immortality" because he saw "revolving life,"[8] because he focused on that which constantly recurs, looking

> *Through* meagre lines and colours, and the press
> Of self-destroying, transitory things.[9]

He looks at that which is permanent even in its mutability, on that which has been, is, and will be. That, after all, is the significance of his interest in the things of common life, in the fundamental, ever-recurring elements in human and external nature.

> And less
> Than other minds I had been used to owe
> The pleasure which I found in place or thing
> To extrinsic transitory accidents,
> Of record or tradition; but a sense
> Of what had been here done, and suffer'd here
> Through ages, and was doing, suffering, still
> Weigh'd with me, could support the test of thought.[1]

What was it that the Solitary Reaper sang? Perhaps of

8. *The Ruined Cottage*, l. 151, 5, 382.
9. *The Prelude*, VII, 738–9. Italics mine.
1. Ibid., VIII, 776–83.

> Some natural sorrow, loss, or pain,
> That has been, and may be again?

The maiden sang as if her song could have no ending, for her singing is a spot of time, a type and symbol of eternity. Such songs will always be sung, and there will always be such maidens to sing them.

Wordsworth's emphasis on the large cyclical view, his sweeping aside of self-destroying, transitory things, is the aspect of his attitude which earns for him Coleridge's epithet *"Spectator ab extra."* [2] Wordsworth even sees himself as a recurring moment in the larger process when he speaks

> Of youthful Poets, who among these hills
> Will be my second self when I am gone.[3]

At the beginning of Book VIII in *The Prelude,* Wordsworth looks down on his beloved vale from the eminence of Mount Helvellyn. From this *ab extra,* godlike point of view, Wordsworth describes a summer fair. The physical distance makes all the participants seem merely typical; the spiritual distance makes the entire event seem typical, a moment in the recurring cycle of that which has been and will be again.

> What sounds are those, Helvellyn, which are heard
> Up to thy summit? Through the depth of air
> Ascending, as if distance had the power
> To make the sounds more audible: what Crowd
> Is yon, assembled in the gay green Field?
> Crowd seems it, solitary Hill! to thee,
> Though but a little Family of Men,
> Twice twenty, with their Children and their Wives,
> And here and there a Stranger interspers'd.

2. Cf. *Table Talk,* July 31, 1832, and Wordsworth, 5, 365.
3. "Michael," ll. 38–9.

It is a summer festival, a Fair,
Such as, on this side now, and now on that,
Repeated through his tributary Vales,
Helvellyn, in the silence of his rest,
Sees annually, if storms be not abroad,
And mists have left him an unshrouded head.

. . . . .

Booths are there none; a Stall or two is here,
A lame Man, or a blind, the one to beg,
The other to make music; hither, too,
From far, with Basket, slung upon her arm,
Of Hawker's Wares, books, pictures, combs, and pins,
Some aged Woman finds her way again,
Year after year a punctual visitant! [4]

The cyclical view is the large view of the temporal-eternal. Within this large view which is focused on the whole, there is a concomitant emphasis on the individual mind. Within the constant pattern of cyclic recurrence there is development and change. And the character of this development is also temporal-eternal. Even within the larger pattern things change and remain the same. This third aspect of the temporal-eternal vision might be called "the doctrine of nonradical development."

Nonradical development gives abundant recompense for the loss which change brings. What is the change? As presented in "Tintern Abbey," it is a change from immediacy to mediation. In youth, the forms of nature evoked a direct, immediate feeling of joy. In maturity, these same forms, coupled with a remembrance of immediate joy, evoke a quieter joy which is mediated by thought and human experience. In maturity, what *was* felt *is* understood consciously, in relation to the whole of things. Emotive, unconscious understanding gives way to an understanding

4. *The Prelude,* VIII, 1–15, 25–31.

which consciously relates man to nature, which relates thought and experience to the original, immediate intuition.

> The sounding cataract
> Haunted me like a passion; the tall rock,
> The mountain, and the deep and gloomy wood,
> Their colours and their forms, were then to me
> An *appetite;* a *feeling* and a *love,*
> That had no need of a *remoter* charm,
> By thought supplied, nor any interest
> Unborrowed from the eye.[5]

With the sanction of what he once felt, the poet looks upon the same forms and feels a joy which has been chastened and subdued by human experience. Experience provides new relational categories and a wider perspective. Now the poet explicitly relates man to nature; he has ideas about the cosmos. But these relational ideas are founded upon the original, immediate feelings of joy; they represent, in fact, a development of those feelings. The sense sublime of something far more deeply interfused is an explicit interpretation of the meaning that was implicit in the immediate joys of childhood. Thus, the new visit to the scene of earlier experience becomes a renewal on a different level of the earlier affirmation. In the new visit the poet is assured that in an important sense all three are the same: the child, the scene, and the man. The man is the explicit result of that which the child was implicitly. The development has been that of growth from a germ. The flower was implicit in the seed. Such periodic renewals as "Tintern Abbey" celebrates (whether they be actual, as in the poem, or remembered, as the poem predicts will be the case in the future) are important. Such renewals prevent us from forgetting the source of our insights; they keep us on the

5. "Tintern Abbey," ll. 76–83. Italics mine.

path of our true, organic development. The man unfolds out of his former self. Seed and flower remain, in a sense, identical. The child is father of the man.

This development is, then, analogous to the larger cycle within which it occurs. The cycle is that of enduring life, birth, growth, death, rebirth—the change which is ever the same. Nonradical development asserts that the stages not only constantly recur, but that they remain essentially the same. As Schelling poetically expresses it. "The flower of eternity unfolds in the temporal." This eternal essence, Schelling deliberately compares to a seed. "Here the universe sleeps as in an infinitely fruitful seed together with the overflowing of its forms, the richness of its life, and the abundance of its developments. These are endless in time but yet completely present in that eternal unity, past and present. For the finite all these are endless; here they are together, unseparated, under a common husk." In another place, Schelling speaks of the world as "one plant in which everything, leaves, flowers, and fruit, are all different not in essence, but only in stage." [6]

Things are different not in essence, but in stage—that is the meaning of change for both Wordsworth and Schelling, the fundamental meaning of nonradical development. All are part of the cyclic pattern of life within which any point is in essence the same as any other point. Is that not one of the central meanings in *The Prelude*? The growth of a poet's mind is truly a growth. "Fair seed-time had my soul" says Wordsworth in Book I.[7] It is the vision of nonradical development which makes a genetic study of the mind important. The end is implicit in the beginning, and the beginning sanctions the truth of Wordsworth's understanding of himself all along the way. In the infant babe he sees "the first Poetic spirit of our human life," the spirit

6. 2, 377; *4*, 258–9, 314.
7. *The Prelude*, I, 305.

which is made explicit and self-conscious in the mature poet. The study of early instincts presents us with the key to later, more advanced processes. The essence is the same, only the stage is different. Wordsworth scorns those who

> class the cabinet
> Of their sensations, and, in voluble phrase,
> Run through the history and birth of each,
> As of a single independent thing.
> Hard task to analyse a soul, in which,
> Not only general habits and desires,
> But each most obvious and particular thought,
> Not in a mystical and idle sense,
> But in the words of reason deeply weigh'd,
> Hath no beginning.[8]

That is precisely the notion of mental development which Schelling asserts. Mind, like everything else, displays the pattern of organic, nonradical development. The *System of Transcendental Idealism* is an elaborate disquisition in philosophical categories of the central notion of mental development in *The Prelude*. In the mind, "the successive series is simply a *development* of an absolute synthesis." "Succession is, as we know, nothing other than the *evolution* of the original and absolute synthesis." [9] For this reason, Schelling feels that he can trace the "epochs" of consciousness without reference to the accidental contingencies of empirical experience. He sees a necessary evolution from immediate sensory experience to reflection in much the same way that Wordsworth perceives a necessary development from one stage to another. A book heading like "Love of Nature Leading to Love of Man" exemplifies this spirit in the poem.

Nonradical development becomes, then, inevitable de-

8. Ibid., II, 275–6, 228–37.
9. Schelling, *3*, 484, 485.

velopment. (The necessary qualification of this point will be found in the chapter on Imagination.) Development becomes the path of implicit destiny. There "arises in us the idea of a teleology for the whole. . . . The series of causes and effects ceases, and we perceive instead a reciprocal tying together of means and end." [1] This teleology is nothing other than the divine purpose within the divine life which realizes itself in nature and in the mind of man:

> I had been taught to reverence a Power
> That is the very quality and shape
> And image of right reason, that matures
> Her processes by steadfast laws, gives birth
> To no impatient or fallacious hopes,
> No heat of passion or excessive zeal,
> No vain conceits, provokes to no quick turns
> Of self-applauding intellect, but lifts
> The Being into magnanimity;
> Holds up before the mind, intoxicate
> With present objects and the busy dance
> Of things that pass away, a temperate shew
> Of objects that endure, and by this course
> Disposes her, when over-fondly set
> On leaving her incumbrances behind
> To seek in Man, and in the frame of life,
> Social and individual, what there is
> Desirable, affecting, good or fair
> Of kindred permanence, the gifts divine
> And universal, the pervading grace
> That hath been, is, and shall be.

Even caught in the seeming chaos of the French Revolution, Wordsworth could say,

> And to the ultimate repose of things
> I look'd with unabated confidence.[2]

1. *Ibid.*, 2, 54.
2. *The Prelude*, XII, 24–44; X, 580–1.

The development of human history is part of the same larger temporal-eternal process in which the individual participates. Human history, as envisioned by the early Schelling, is a cycle with three stages, Nature, Fate, and Providence. "These three ideas express in different ways the same identity. Fate is also Providence—seen in the real, just as Providence is Fate perceived in the ideal. The eternal necessity reveals itself at the time of identity with itself as Nature." [3] Human life is like the inevitable progress from dawn to dusk. It is cyclical, inevitable, and it expresses the divine purpose. "And stepping westward seemed to be A kind of *heavenly* destiny":

> I liked the greeting; 'twas a sound
> Of something without place or bound.[4]

The temporal-eternal view of things which I have sketched is, I think, crucial in Wordsworth's poetry of the Great Decade and in Schelling's philosophy of a like period. By crucial I mean to say that the view is at once essential to Enthusiasm and an extremely difficult view to sustain. Neither Schelling nor Wordsworth was able to sustain it. This is not surprising. One of man's universal experiences would seem to be that of the radical nature of change in human life. Sooner or later, time itself destroys the notion that in human experience time somehow is not. At this point a man has two basic alternatives: he can give up the idea of eternity altogether or he can preserve both time and eternity as existing in two distinct realms. A third possibility would seem to be the Parmenidean denial of time, but in that case one also denies life, for it is impossible to conceive of life as real if time is mere illusion. This third choice was hardly open to Wordsworth and Schelling, since what forced them to give up the temporal-eternal

3. 5, 290.
4. "Stepping Westward," ll. 11–14.

view was not an experience of time's illusoriness but rather the experience of its radical nature.

Schelling chose the first path. The unchanged and unchanging disappears from his philosophy after about 1809. In this shift he was prompted perhaps by Hegel's *Phenomenology* which he began reading upon its publication in 1807.[5] For Schelling the problem of time was resolved by making time itself a category just as fundamental as Being. Being is conceived of as Becoming. In later works the notion of substance is itself a temporal notion. Substance is process. God is a temporal God; He is Becoming. Schelling retains the idea that world is God's reality, but this reality is no longer temporal-eternal. It is no longer a circle but a straight line. No longer is each moment absolute because it is in some sense eternal; rather the absolute is *in* the moment. (Before, you will remember, Schelling saw each moment as *in* God.) The absolute is now itself temporal. The past is absorbed in the present; the future is not yet.

Wordsworth's choice was the one that had been made by St. Augustine when he witnessed the sack of "eternal" Rome. When Augustine wrote *The City of God* he solved the problem involving the relationship of time and eternity by asserting a radical distinction between the two. There is time for man and time for God. Time for man is successive, absolutely temporal. Man cannot transcend this temporality in his earthly existence. Time for God is not. For God alone is there absolute eternity, and only God holds the synthesis of the two. The synthesis is there, but not for man's experience nor his intellect. There is a radical distinction between the city of God and the city of man. In his own way, Wordsworth accepted such a solution. And this acceptance implies an acute shift in the poet's spiritual outlook. The distinction between human

5. Cf. Plitt, *Aus Schellings Leben*, 2, 124. See, also, my remarks at the end of the chapter on Imagination.

life and eternity implies other radical distinctions all along the way, not the least important being the radical distinction between God and the world. A shift in attitude toward time implies for Wordsworth a shift from panentheism to theism.

An examination of two poems will, I think, make these assertions clear. The first is a typical piece appearing in the 1800 edition of *Lyrical Ballads*. It is "The Two April Mornings," written in 1799. In my discussion of this poem, some of the points I have made about Wordsworth's temporal-eternal view will be brought together. The second poem was written in 1805, and, to my mind, marks the end of Wordsworth's Great Decade. This poem, the "Elegiac Stanzas," was written in connection with the death of Wordsworth's brother, John. Here Wordsworth states explicitly that a change has occurred in his point of view. The poet himself seems to corroborate de Selincourt's idea that John's death occasioned a fundamental change in Wordsworth's outlook and poetry.[6] I shall try to show that this fundamental change is directly connected with the poet's idea of time: that his change of outlook involves a rejection of the temporal-eternal perspective. The significance of the contrast between the two poems is that it shows the temporal-eternal idea of time to be essential to the earlier poetry, and it shows the rejection of that idea to be characteristic of the poet's later viewpoint.

The Two April Mornings

We walked along, while bright and red
Uprose the morning sun;
And Matthew stopped, he looked, and said,
"The will of God be done!"

6. Cf. de Selincourt, *The Prelude*, p. 608. Harper makes this point even more powerfully: "The Crisis in Wordsworth's Life and Art," *Queen's Quarterly, 40* (1933), 1–13.

A village schoolmaster was he,
With hair of glittering grey;
As blithe a man as you could see
On a spring holiday.

And on that morning, through the grass,
And by the steaming rills,
We travelled merrily, to pass
A day among the hills.

"Our work," said I, "was well begun,
Then, from thy breast what thought,
Beneath so beautiful a sun,
So sad a sigh has brought?"

A second time did Matthew stop;
And fixing still his eye
Upon the eastern mountain-top,
To me he made reply:

"Yon cloud with that long purple cleft
Brings fresh into my mind
A day like this which I have left
Full thirty years behind.

"And just above yon slope of corn
Such colours, and no other,
Were in the sky, that April morn,
Of this the very brother.

"With rod and line I sued the sport
Which that sweet season gave,
And, to the churchyard come, stopped short
Beside my daughter's grave.

"Nine summers had she scarcely seen,
The pride of all the vale;
And then she sang;—she would have been
A very nightingale.

"Six feet in earth my Emma lay;
And yet I loved her more,
For so it seemed, than till that day
I e'er had loved before.

"And, turning from her grave, I met,
Beside the churchyard yew,
A blooming Girl, whose hair was wet
With points of morning dew.

"A basket on her head she bare;
Her brow was smooth and white:
To see a child so very fair,
It was a pure delight!

"No fountain from its rocky cave
E'er tripped with foot so free;
She seemed as happy as a wave
That dances on the sea.

"There came from me a sigh of pain
Which I could ill confine;
I looked at her, and looked again:
And did not wish her mine!"

Matthew is in his grave, yet now,
Methinks, I see him stand,
As at that moment, with a bough
Of wilding in his hand.

This is a poem which refers to death and change in human life, yet its spirit is affirmative. Matthew himself, certainly, does not seem to affirm anything explicitly. He sighs; he seems resigned: "The will of God be done!" He seems to be inconsolable:

I looked at her and looked again
And did not wish her mine.

Those lines mean, I think, that Matthew could not accept the "blooming Girl" as a substitute for his daughter, as in:

> "And, Matthew, for thy children dead
> I'll be a son to thee!"
> At this he grasped my hand, and said,
> "Alas! that cannot be." [7]

What has been taken away can never be restored; his loss has touched him deeply. Yet, in spite of his resignation and his sighs, he is

> As blithe a man as you could see
> On a spring holiday.

It would seem that Matthew is somehow consoled even though he is not completely aware of the fact. Somehow his loss has not been irreparable. He still finds joy in life; he is still a lover of the rills and mountains. He still likes traveling "merrily to pass a day among the hills." Perhaps this joy compensates to an extent for his loss. But why should nature console him, even unconsciously?

It will be noted that the milieu in which the poet places Matthew and himself is highly selective. It consists almost exclusively of typical natural forms, forms which are unchanging or which always recur. The first image is that of the morning sun rising. The poet and Matthew pass through the grass ("as constant as the grass upon the fields"). They go by the steaming rills:

> "No check, no stay, this Streamlet fears;
> How merrily it goes!
> 'Twill murmur on a thousand years,
> And flow as now it flows." [8]

---

7. "The Fountain," ll. 61–4.
8. "The Fountain," ll. 21–4.

The two of them are "to pass a day among the hills"; Matthew gazes at the mountain top. (Hills and mountains are, of course, Wordsworth's permanent forms par excellence.) Matthew looks at a cloud. (Clouds are always there, even though they alter, and this particular cloud reminds Matthew of one he had seen before.) He looks at a "slope of corn," which in the first printed version was a "slope of springing corn." The crops come up every year with the recurring seasons. The seasons themselves are explicitly mentioned, April, "nine summers," "that sweet season." Matthew's daughter is spoken of as the pride of the "vale." She lies "six feet in earth." Matthew's encounter with the blooming girl occurs beside a yew tree ("a living thing Produced too slowly ever to decay").[9] The girl herself is compared to a fountain (cf. the lines above quoted from "The Fountain"). She is compared to a wave on the sea, reminding one of Novalis' favorite image for the whole of life. The waves move, and they remain part of the sea which is ever the same.

Just as typical and permanent are the elements in human life referred to in the poem. They are all connected with general and permanent experiences, with "the operations of the elements, and the appearances of the visible universe; with storm and sunshine, with the revolutions of the seasons, with cold and heat, with loss of friends and kindred . . ."[1] The human elements which Wordsworth selects are all of the sort which have always been and always will be. Matthew is a "village schoolmaster," as blithe as though he were on a "spring holiday." He likes to walk, to fish. He visits the "churchyard" and his "daughter's grave." Like the Solitary Reaper, his daughter sang. Matthew loved her; he expresses sorrow that he has lost her.

9. "Yew-trees," ll. 10–11.

1. From the preface to the 1800 edition of *Lyrical Ballads*, in Wordsworth, 2, 397.

The girl Matthew meets is a typical, not a special, "blooming Girl." (It is significant that "Girl" is capitalized, whereas none of the other ordinary nouns is.) The girl has few individual characteristics; her skin is smooth; her hair is wet with morning dew. She is *youth.* She, like all other things human in the poem, will always be. And so is the poet *youth,* as he accompanies Matthew. The two walk together, the old man "With hair of glittering grey" and the young poet. Youth and age are side by side. The stages of life ever come and go, yet they remain. And although Matthew has lost his daughter, there is, even if he is not consoled by the fact, the young girl with a basket on her head. Life with all its stages remains. Even Matthew's expression of sorrow is one of those "general thoughts and feelings" which always have been and always will be.[2]

Matthew is blithe because the permanent and recurrent forms in nature and in human life are intertwined with his life. Their beauty, constancy, divinity have a secret effect upon him. Matthew's life (as described in the poem) is led exclusively amid the elements of nature and human life which deny radical loss. The very occasion for the renewal of his sorrow is an event which points to the permanent, cyclic nature of things, just as in "Tintern Abbey" the occasion of the poet's awareness of change in himself is an event which in itself denies radical change. Matthew is reminded of his loss because the second April morning is a repetition of the morning when he felt his loss most deeply, a morning he had left "full thirty years behind." Human life and natural cyclicity are types of one another.

> that April morn,
> Of this the very brother.

The mornings are like Wordsworth and his sister in "Tintern Abbey"; they are the same, only each is at a dif-

2. Ibid.

ferent stage, a different point in time. Human life and
natural cyclicity intertwine when Matthew says,

> I sued the sport
> Which that sweet season gave.

Almost every element in the poem points to that which is
permanent and/or cyclic.[3]

The final stanza has reference to a later point in time.
Now, in writing the poem, the mature poet remembers
the second April morning with its references to a similar
April morning before the birth of the poet himself. Now
Matthew is dead and the poet is older. By the power of
memory and imagination, the occasion of the poem becomes a repetition of that second April morning. "Matthew is in his grave," yet the poet imagines him "as at that
moment, with a bough of wilding in his hand." The bough
of wilding again associates Matthew with nature, and he
becomes a human form which, like the natural forms, will
always be. The poet himself *continues* in his imagination
that natural process which does not permit uncompensated
loss. The poet, sustained by the temporal-eternal pattern
which he intuits in nature and in human life (that second
April morning was a spot of time), can, in his mind, see,
feel, imagine Matthew to be there forever as he was at that
moment. For Matthew, the individual, is also a type and
a symbol of eternity, a man whose life is lived in connection with "the operations of the elements" etc., a man who
always has been and will be. The poet sees his experience
as part of an eternal process, and the poem itself points to
the process as a whole. In spite of all seeming change, the
constant goodness and rightness in the tide of things has
been affirmed.

The "Elegiac Stanzas" refer, likewise, to time and

---

3. Human life imposes something on nature as well as vice versa; cf.
"Poems on the Naming of Places."

change. The poet contemplates a picture representing a
scene that has been familiar to him. He contrasts the
quality of the scene as he knew it and would have painted
it, with its quality as depicted in the actual painting, and
he points out that this contrast is like the contrast between
his present self and his former self. The poet accepts the
interpretation of the scene which he finds in the painting,
and he rejects his own memory of the scene. In like fashion,
he accepts a new spiritual attitude and rejects the attitude
of his former self as being pitiably blind. The structure of
the poem reflects the contrast being made; it divides in the
middle. The first thirty-two lines are concerned with characterizing the former idea of Peele Castle and, implicitly,
the feelings and attitudes of the poet's former self. From
line 33 to the end the poet describes, in striking contrast to
the earlier idea, the present painting, and characterizes
the radical change which he has undergone. It is hardly
necessary to point out that this uncompromising rejection
of the poet's former self is in striking contrast to the pervasive child-is-father-of-the-man motif in Wordsworth's
earlier poetry. As far as I know, this is the only example
in Wordsworth of symmetrical opposition in the structure
of a poem.

Elegiac Stanzas

Suggested by a Picture of Peele Castle, in a Storm, Painted by Sir George Beaumont

I was thy neighbour once, thou rugged Pile!
Four summer weeks I dwelt in sight of thee:
I saw thee every day; and all the while
Thy Form was sleeping on a glassy sea.

So pure the sky, so quiet was the air!
So like, so very like, was day to day!

Whene'er I looked, thy Image still was there;
It trembled, but it never passed away.

How perfect was the calm! it seemed no sleep;
No mood, which season takes away, or brings:
I could have fancied that the mighty Deep
Was even the gentlest of all gentle Things.

Ah! THEN, if mine had been the Painter's hand,
To express what then I saw; and add the gleam,
The light that never was, on sea or land,
The consecration, and the Poet's dream;

I would have planted thee, thou hoary Pile
Amid a world how different from this!
Beside a sea that could not cease to smile;
On tranquil land, beneath a sky of bliss.

Thou shouldst have seemed a treasure-house divine
Of peaceful years; a chronicle of heaven;—
Of all the sunbeams that did ever shine
The very sweetest had to thee been given.

A Picture had it been of lasting ease,
Elysian quiet, without toil or strife;
No motion but the moving tide, a breeze,
Or merely silent Nature's breathing life.

Such, in the fond illusion of my heart,
Such Picture would I at that time have made:
And seen the soul of truth in every part,
A stedfast peace that might not be betrayed.

So once it would have been,—'tis so no more;
I have submitted to a new control:
A power is gone, which nothing can restore;
A deep distress hath humanised my Soul.

Not for a moment could I now behold
A smiling sea, and be what I have been:

The feeling of my loss will ne'er be old;
This, which I know, I speak with mind serene.

Then, Beaumont, Friend! who would have been the
    Friend,
If he had lived, of Him whom I deplore,
This work of thine I blame not, but commend;
This sea in anger, and that dismal shore.

O 'tis a passionate Work!—yet wise and well,
Well chosen is the spirit that is here;
That Hulk which labours in the deadly swell,
This rueful sky, this pageantry of fear!

And this huge Castle, standing here sublime,
I love to see the look with which it braves,
Cased in the unfeeling armour of old time,
The lightning, the fierce wind, and trampling waves.

Farewell, farewell the heart that lives alone,
Housed in a dream, at distance from the Kind!
Such happiness, wherever it be known,
Is to be pitied; for 'tis surely blind.

But welcome fortitude, and patient cheer,
And frequent sights of what is to be borne!
Such sights, or worse, as are before me here.—
Not without hope we suffer and we mourn.

The early view of Peele Castle is that of a changeless form reflected by a peaceful sea. The peace is, however, not altogether static. There is "tumult and peace" together. The image "trembled, but it never passed away"; it is an image like "silent nature's breathing life." The form is not lifeless; it *sleeps* on the glassy sea. The calm and peace which Wordsworth describes is the calm of life taken as a whole, the round ocean, rather than its waves. Schelling's comment is descriptive: "Whoever could find expression for an activity which is peaceful as the deepest calm, for a calmness which is active as the highest activity would come close to the nature of the all-complete." [4] The scene is an image of the temporal-eternal, at once activity and calm.

But calm is emphasized more than activity. In his remembered image, the poet sees "A stedfast peace that might not be betrayed." To understand the nature of this emphasis, the analogy of spatial distance is useful. The image of Peele Castle's trembling reflection can only be gained when the observer stands at a vantage point far enough away from the reflection to see it as a whole. Suppose that instead of viewing the castle and the sea from a distance, the observer views the sea from a closer position. Suppose he were in a boat in the midst of the reflected form. Then, instead of seeing an image mirrored by the surface, he would see the waves themselves; the reflection would become a jumble of moving, luminous points. The implied physical distance in the first stanzas expresses a spiritual distance like that in the passage which describes Mount Helvellyn towering above the summer fair. The poet sees the whole, and this whole seems to have

> No motion but the moving tide, a breeze,
> Or merely silent Nature's breathing life.

If we take Peele Castle itself as a symbol of human life, the picture which Wordsworth paints in the first half of the poem becomes highly significant. The Castle seems to Wordsworth

> a treasure-house divine
> Of peaceful years; a chronicle of heaven.

This is suggestive of Wordsworth's "Address" to his infant daughter, where her life is seen as a chronicle of heaven.

---

4. *4,* 305. For further examples of Wordsworth's characteristic use of reflections, see Ch. 6.

> But what is time? What outward glory? Neither
> A measure is of Thee, whose claims extend
> Through "heaven's eternal year." [5]

Peele Castle is like the constant cycle of human life as a whole, within which the "peaceful years" of human activity take their course. This constant (temporal-eternal) form is reflected in the "eternal motion" [6] of the sea, just as human life stands in a reciprocal relation to the temporal-eternal processes of nature.

This reciprocal relation is also an "interfusion." Both the castle, standing "on tranquil land," and the "sea that could not cease to smile" are united "beneath a sky of bliss." The smile of the sea, the bliss of the whole scene is expressed by light. The smile of the sea is the sunlight reflected by the waves. To the castle itself is given

> Of all the sunbeams that did ever shine
> The very sweetest.

The light which covers the whole scene is like "the pervading grace That hath been, is, and shall be," [7] the universal principle of joy and divine self-affirmation. It is this universal principle which the poet intuits with his imaginative faculty, and perceives as suffusing the whole scene. The poet adds explicitly the pervasive joy implicit in the world process; he adds

> the gleam,
> The light that never was, on sea or land,
> The consecration and the Poet's dream.

The imagination of the poet is, then, comparable to the sky of bliss. It unites the whole scene and illuminates it with a confident spirit of affirmation. The poet would have painted such a picture because he was then confident that

5. "Address to my Infant Daughter, Dora," ll. 13–15.
6. Cf. "It is a beauteous evening," l. 7.
7. *The Prelude,* XII, 43–4.

> the mighty Deep
> Was even the gentlest of all gentle things.

By this confidence in the gentleness of things, in the goodness and rightness of the world process (symbolized here as
elsewhere by the sea), the poet *consecrates* what he sees
with the light of imagination. He transfigures everything
with the principle of joy inherent in the whole. His light
is like the divine, gentle purpose which he intuits as shin-
ing through the temporal-eternal nature of things. The
poet's dream and the sky of bliss come together. His spiritual distance is like the encompassing remoteness of the
divine illumination.

It is this remoteness in his soul which Wordsworth in
the subsequent stanzas rejects as illusion:

> Such, in the fond illusion of my heart,
> Such picture would I at that time have made.

Humanity, and the human point of view are now brought
into an opposition with the joyful distance of his earlier
self.

> So once it would have been—'tis so no more;
> I have submitted to a new control:
> A power is gone which nothing can restore;
> A deep distress hath humanized my Soul.

> Not for a moment could I now behold
> A smiling sea, and be what I have been.

The joyful remoteness of the poet's viewpoint gave him a
power which he now associates with spiritual isolation.
Only in such isolation, "at distance from the Kind," was it
possible to view the course of human life as unchanging in
its change, as a "chronicle of heaven." The former viewpoint *necessitated* a spiritual solitude. The sense of kinship with and love of humanity had to be a general, contemplative love, for a fervent attachment to an individual

human being would imply that the individual has an absolute, not just a typical, value. The poet can no longer confidently say,

> Thy love is human merely; this proceeds
> More from the brooding Soul, and is divine.[8]

Bidding adieu to the "divine" perspective, Wordsworth says,

> Farewell, farewell the heart that lives alone,
> Housed in a dream, at distance from the Kind!
> Such happiness, wherever it be known,
> Is to be pitied, for 'tis surely blind.

Before, the "Poet's dream" seemed to provide a vision into the bright truth of things. Now, being "housed in a dream" is synonymous with blindness.

The event which caused the poet's rejection of his former viewpoint and brought about his present feeling of solidarity with the rest of humanity was the death of someone he dearly loved. The former viewpoint denied radical loss; the poet's bereavement *is* a radical loss: "The feeling of my loss will ne'er be old." An experience stronger than the experience of pervasive goodness has proved irresistible. The poet finds himself drawn permanently closer to concrete, particular human feelings, and this closeness makes the pattern disappear. The reflection of the castle is gone. There are now only waves, the hulk of a ship, and a "rueful sky." The poet's position is now, so to speak, on the ship itself, for now the scene presents a "pageantry of fear."

With the loss of joyful distance, the poet necessarily loses the temporal-eternal view of things. Peele Castle is like a man whom experience has "Cased in the unfeeling armour of old time." Human life is no longer a chronicle of

8. Ibid., XIII, 164-5.

heaven; it is a sturdy hulk which, like the castle, braves
"The lightning, the fierce wind, and trampling [!] waves."
These things are "deadly"; they are not gentle "moments
in the being Of the eternal Silence"; battered by them,
one does not have "soothing thoughts that spring Out of
human suffering." [9] One has "fortitude, and patient
cheer." The cheer is patient; it awaits something, and it
is what man *awaits* that makes him cheerful, which grants
him fortitude; it is not what man somehow has, here and
now.

"Not without hope we suffer and we mourn." The hope
is for a fulfillment or compensation in a realm other than
this world, the world in which, as the earlier Wordsworth

9. Immortality Ode, ll. 155–6, 184–5. Compare the description here with
a tempest from the "temporal-eternal" period (MS lines, *The Prelude*,
p. 601):

> It was a day
> Upon the edge of Autumn, fierce with storm;
> The wind blew through the hills of Coniston
> Compress'd as in a tunnel, from the lake
> Bodies of foam took flight, and the whole vale
> Was wrought into commotion high and low—
> Mist flying up and down, bewilder'd showers,
> Ten thousand thousand waves, mountains and crags,
> And darkness, and the sun's tumultuous light.
> Green leaves were rent in handfuls from the trees,
> The mountains all seem'd silent, din so near
> Pealed in the traveller's ear, the clouds
> The horse and rider stagger'd in the blast,
> And he who look'd upon the stormy lake
> Had fear for boat or vessel where none was.
> Meanwhile, by what strange chance I cannot tell,
> What combination of the wind and clouds,
> A large unmutilate(d) rainbow stood
> Immoveable in heav'n, kept standing there
> With a colossal stride bridging the vale,
> The substance thin as dreams, lovelier than day,—
> Amid the deafening uproar stood unmov'd,
> Sustain'd itself through many minutes space;
> As if it were pinn'd down by adamant.

said, "we find our happiness or not at all." [1] In this world we suffer and we mourn. All is *not* compensated for, all is *not* presently good; time and change *are* radical. The poet, now in the midst of time, looks "with mind serene" toward the eternal city of God.

1. *The Prelude,* X, 728.

6. Imagination

There is nothing of me that is alone and absolute except in my mind, and we shall find that the mind has no existence by itself, it is only the glitter of the sun on the surface of the waters. So that my individualism is really an illusion. I am part of the great whole, and I can never escape. But I can deny my connections, break them and become a fragment. Then I am wretched.

D. H. Lawrence *

ENTHUSIASM NEEDS to find concepts and categories which support and sustain its experience. In previous chapters I have tried to delineate the principal notions which Enthusiasm uses to support its world. These have been, for the most part, notions which concern the nature of reality; they have tended to be metaphysical rather than epistemological. But Enthusiasm needs to support its experience epistemologically. It cannot take its knowledge for granted, since its knowledge seems to be at odds with ordinary logic and common sense. Enthusiasm seems everywhere to deny the logical postulates, $A = A$ and $A \neq$ not-A. Indeed, A seems everywhere to be not-A as well. Enthusiasm has to find a logic of its own, which will validate its knowledge.

---

* From *Apocalypse*. By permission of the Viking Press, Inc.

This is nothing other than the logic of "life": Imagination is like Hegel's *Logik:* it is a living dialectic.

The dialectical pattern is the structural constant of Imagination, which gives the term a unified meaning throughout all the diverse functions of the imaginative process. For, Imagination is first and foremost an activity, not a static pattern. Yet its activity always follows a pattern of interaction or reciprocity. Some of Wordsworth's expressions have led to confusion on this point, as Wellek and others have pointed out.

> Wordsworth disconcertingly vacillates among three epistemological conceptions. At times he makes imagination purely subjective, an imposition of the human mind on the real world. At other times he makes it an illumination beyond the control of the conscious mind and even beyond the individual soul. But most frequently he takes an in-between position which favors the idea of a collaboration.[1]

Schelling, too, sometimes seems to vacillate in this way, as I noted earlier in speaking of "Intellectual Intuition." The true nature of such vacillation is, I think, understandable in the context of my previous discussion.[2] When Wordsworth and Schelling speak of an illumination beyond consciousness and individual control, they do not describe the typical active reciprocity of Enthusiasm but rather its temporary (and necessary) moment of fusion. That is not Imagination but a moment within the activity of Imagination, a moment of static fulfillment. When, on the other hand, "the mind Is lord and master," [3] we are dealing with another necessary but atypical moment. This

1. René Wellek, *A History of Modern Criticism: 1750—1950,* Vol. 2: *The Romantic Age* (New Haven, Yale Univ. Press, 1955), p. 145.
2. Cf. ch. 5, p. 66 ff.
3. *The Prelude,* XI, ll. 272-3.

subjective imposition is related to "Fancy" or *reine Phan-tasie,* and I discuss this activity further on in this chapter. Neither mystic fusion nor subjective imposition is an example of Imagination itself, and I know of no passage where Wordsworth equates these moments with Imagination. The passages which lead to that impression are not assertions but equivocations:

> My seventeenth year was come
> And, whether from this habit, rooted now
> So deeply in my mind, or from excess
> Of the great social principle of life,
> Coercing all things into sympathy,
> To unorganic natures I transferr'd
> My own enjoyments, or, the power of truth
> Coming in revelation, I convers'd
> With things that really are, I, at this time
> Saw blessings spread around me like a sea.

Another example:

> —To these emotions, whencesoe'er they come,
> Whether from breath of outward circumstance,
> Or from the Soul—an impulse to herself—
> I would give utterance in numerous verse.[4]

The terms *whether—or* provide the essential clue. Such equivocations are concessions to ordinary logic. I should like to think that neither alternative expresses the truth of the case, but, rather, that both "alternatives" must be stated at once. For Imagination itself is precisely the activity which unites opposites that seem to be mutually exclusive.

What, then, is that wonderful faculty which can, ac

4. *The Prelude,* II, 405–14; prospectus to *The Recluse,* ll. 10–13.

cording to the philosopher, overcome an infinite opposition by productive perception? Up to now we have not been able to make this mechanism fully comprehensible, because only the artistic faculty can completely unveil it. Through that productive faculty art, too, attains the impossible by overcoming an infinite opposition in a finite product. It is the poetic faculty, and this is, in its first potency, original perception. Conversely, it is simply productive perception repeating itself in its highest potency which we call the poetic faculty. One and the same function characterizes both. That function is the unique means by which we can think and grasp as a unity that which is contradictory—Imagination.[5]

Imagination is never one-sided. It was the notion of subjective imposition that made Schelling take up arms against Kant. And it was Kant's own concept of *Einbildungskraft* which Schelling transformed to use as one of his main weapons.[6] Kant's notion of subjective imposition seemed to separate thought and being into distinct realms. Before being can become intelligible to us, it must be made to conform to the mind's categories. Thus Kant:

Hitherto it has been assumed that all our knowledge must conform to objects. But all attempts to extend our knowledge of objects by establishing something in regard to them *a priori,* by means of concepts, have, on this assumption, ended in failure. We must there-

5. Schelling, *3*, 626.
6. It will be remembered that, for Kant, *Einbildungskraft* is a function which effects a subsumption of sense intuition under the categories of understanding, in order that we may have knowledge. It is neither sense nor thought, but a third thing, similar to both. Cf. *The Critique of Pure Reason*, A137–8, B176–7.

fore make trial whether we may not have more suc-
cess in the tasks of metaphysics, if we suppose that
objects must conform to our knowledge.[7]

Wordsworth and Schelling demand that both postulates be
made at once. Imagination brings thought and being together in an active, reciprocal unity:

> my voice proclaims
> How exquisitely the individual Mind
> (And the progressive powers perhaps no less
> Of the whole species) to the external World
> Is fitted:—and how exquisitely, too—
> Theme this but little heard of among men—
> The external World is fitted to the Mind;
> And the creation (by no lower name
> Can it be called) which they with blended might
> Accomplish:—this is our high argument.[8]

Thought and being are both expressions of the one life
within us and abroad. Like all expressions of the one life,
they act reciprocally upon one another. "It is obviously
quite useless to ask whether thought or being should
have a preferential status. For neither has any value without the other. Only both together can bring forth the
highest." [9] All oppositions are reconciled in Imagination,
as they are in the one life. For the living Absolute is itself
the ground of all oppositions and the source of all autonomous existence. "The ideal as such is not cause of a deter-
mination in the real, nor is the real cause of a determina-
tion in the ideal. Neither has greater worth, nor is one to
be understood as deriving from the other, since neither at-

7. *The Critique of Pure Reason*, trans. N. K. Smith (London, Macmillan,
1933), p. 22.
8. Prospectus to *The Recluse*, ll. 62–71.
9. Schelling, *3*, 618.

tains the status of a basic principle. Both knowledge and being are reflexes from one and the same Absolute." [1]

The active reciprocity of Imagination is, then, a continuation of the active reciprocity which characterizes the life of things. Imagination is the epistemological sanction for a living universe, and this same universe sanctions the logic of Imagination. Epistemology is grounded in ontology and vice versa. Note the exclamation points in these two characteristic descriptions:

> The swan on still St. Mary's Lake
> Float double, swan and shadow!

> A twofold image; on a grassy bank
> A snow-white ram, and in the crystal flood
> Another and the same! [2]

The object and the reflection are not distinct from one another; the boundary is lost and they form a dialectical unity:

> See yonder the same pageant, and again
> Behold the universal imagery
> Inverted, all its sun-bright features touched
> As with the varnish, and the gloss of dreams;
> Dreamlike the blending also of the whole
> Harmonious landscape; all along the shore
> The boundary lost, the line invisible
> That parts the image from reality;
> And the clear hills, as high as they ascend
> Heavenward, so piercing deep the lake below. [3]

Echoes perform the same function,[4] as do scenes like the following:

1. Ibid., *4*, 304.
2. "Yarrow Unvisited," ll. 43–4; *The Excursion*, IX, ll. 440–2, composed 1804.
3. *The Recluse*, ll. 570–9, *5*, 332.
4. Cf., e.g., "To Joanna," ll. 54–73, and "Stepping Westward," ll. 23–6.

I, so oft,
Had lain awake, on breezy nights, to watch
The moon in splendour couch'd among the leaves
Of a tall ash, that near our cottage stood,
Had watch'd her with fix'd eyes, while to and fro
In the dark summit of the moving Tree
She rock'd with every impulse of the wind.[5]

This is not oscillation from one pole to another. It is an active, reciprocal unity which contains the oppositions within itself, in a scene "Where earth and heaven do make one imagery." [6] These natural scenes provide hints

Of unknown modes of being which on earth,
Or in the heavens, or in the heavens and earth
Exist by mighty combinations, bound
Together by a link, and with a soul
Which makes all one.[7]

Such occasions, where the quality of nature itself exemplifies the activity of Imagination, are, as every Wordsworthian knows, ubiquitous in Wordsworth's poetry. They are types and symbols of the poet's own imaginative relationship to nature. The power in nature which "transforms" opposed elements into a reciprocal unity is the same power which, consciously, "higher minds bear with them as their own."

The Power which these
Acknowledge when thus moved, which Nature thus
Thrusts forth upon the senses, is the express
Resemblance, in the fulness of its strength
Made visible, a genuine Counterpart
And Brother of the glorious faculty

5. *The Prelude*, IV, 77–83.
6. "To H. C. Six Years Old," l. 10.
7. MS poetry, 5, 340–1.

Which higher minds bear with them as their own.
That is the very spirit in which they deal
With all the objects of the universe;
They from their native selves can send abroad
Like transformations, for themselves create
A like existence, and, whene'er it is
Created for them, catch it by an instinct.[8]

Imagination, like life, is characterized by reciprocal activity and, like life, its reciprocal activity is purposeful. It is activity which harmonizes things and moves toward a goal.[9] It strives to unify seemingly diverse elements and, in so striving, it attains the fulfillment it seeks. For, the goal toward which it strives is, in a deeper sense, already attained. The very unity it seeks is that which makes possible its activity of seeking, for thought and being are implicitly unified. The transformed unity which Imagination achieves is an expression of the underlying unity of thought and being which is itself the ground of imaginative activity. But it is a transformed unity; it is now explicit. Just as the plant is an explicit fulfillment of that which was in the seed, so is the act of Imagination an act which makes explicit the implicit unity of all things. Transformation is explicitation.[1] Imagination is life in its most developed form or, as Schelling would say, in its "highest potency." The goal of Imagination is the goal of life, an ever more explicit, articulated expression of life. In relation to this goal, Imagination (or life in its highest potency) represents a fulfillment of the self and a fulfillment of the cosmos. The two goals are one for the same

8. *The Prelude,* XIII, 84–96.
9. Cf. Ch. 4 above.
1. I use the doublet "explicit-explicitation" to emphasize the connection between the two words. The more common verb "to explicate," while it has the same root meaning, has also the undesirable connotation "to explain."

reason that the life in things is also the life through things. The health and development of the organ is dependent upon and, at the same time, necessary to the health and development of the organism. It was necessary to discuss separately (for the purposes of analysis) the life through things and the life in things. In the same way, it will be necessary to analyze separately the quality of Imagination as cosmic and as individual self-fulfillment.

Imagination fulfills the goal of life. It is life in its highest potency. But it is misleading to speak in this way without recalling that every stage in a living, progressive development is, in essence, the same as every other stage. All things in nature are divine; every real natural object expresses something ideal, something holy and good. But this ideality remains inarticulate or "unconscious." In Imagination, the unity of the ideal and the real becomes conscious of itself; it becomes explicit. Imagination is a conscious unity of the real and the ideal. It always has a "pole" which could be characterized as "passive" or "unconscious" and a "pole" which is active or conscious. Imagination achieves an active, conscious unity of thought and being; it is the instrument whereby nature becomes conscious of itself. "Nature begins unconscious and ends conscious," says Schelling.[2] Man's consciousness is the crown of nature. Thus, there seems to be a hierarchy in the stages of Nature's development. Everything has

> its station and its office,
> Through all the mighty commonwealth of things;
> Up from the creeping plant to sovereign Man.[3]

Schelling, likewise, sees "the common life of Nature" as subsisting "in the most varied forms, in progressive stages of development, in the gradual approach to freedom." Yet in spite of man's unique degree of consciousness and free-

2. *3*, 613.
3. *The Excursion*, IV, ll. 341–3, composed 1800.

dom, he is, in essence, not better than nor different from the meanest flower that blows. The profound truth of hierarchy is equality. "Only the Understanding subordinates. In Reason and in Imagination everything is free and moves in the same aether." [4] Imagination recognizes both man's unique glory and his profound equality with other things in nature. Man's imaginative consciousness is the highest attainment of the cosmos because it is the cosmos become aware of itself in the unity of its life.

That is the first aspect of nature's teleological fulfillment. It is Imagination qua *truth,* qua cosmic self-awareness. Schelling says, characteristically, "In Reason Nature contemplates her past works; she perceives and recognizes herself as herself." Man's awareness is Nature's self-consciousness. "Man, the mental being, is placed here to be an enlargement of the cosmos." [5] In man, the divine life becomes divine self-revelation. He was, for Wordsworth, "of all visible natures crown," not because his essence was different but because he was

> first
> In capability of feeling what
> Was to be felt.[6]

This "feeling intellect" is the highest truth of consciousness because here consciousness senses its own true character, namely its fundamental kinship with unconscious reality. Both consciousness and the unconscious are "products of one and the same activity." [7]

> That which in stealth by Nature was performed
> Hath Reason sanctioned.[8]

The purposeful activity of the divine life leads to self-

4. 2, 47–8; 5, 393.
5. 2, 378; 5, 218.
6. *The Prelude,* VIII, 633–5.
7. Schelling, *3,* 626.
8. *The Recluse,* ll. 733–4, 5, 337.

revelation. It is the conscious return of God to Himself. Imagination as truth (i.e. "reason in her most exalted mood") is the self-affirmation of nature in the form of self-knowledge. And because this self-knowledge *is* self-affirmation, it is joy. Truth is nature's self-enjoyment.[9]

But cosmic self-affirmation is not passive self-enjoyment; it is activity. Imagination is the crown of action in this "active universe." Active self-awareness is simply one aspect of life's more inclusive goal. Life *realizes* its goals; they are not fulfilled in the realm of knowledge alone. Philosophical knowledge was for Schelling a union of the ideal and the real in the realm of the ideal. But he always asserted that Imagination effects a conscious union of the two in the real itself, here and now in this glorious world. Man consciously becomes an actual participant in "Nature's holy plan." [1] For both Wordsworth and Schelling, Imagination realizes the goals of life in two realms: the ethical and the aesthetic. The two realms interpenetrate, but I shall discuss them separately.

The cosmos exhibits moral purposiveness. In Prime Nature moral goals are realized unconsciously and necessarily. There the life of the cosmos pushes forward unswervingly in the bosom of God's will. "The eternal necessity," says Schelling, "reveals itself as Nature." [2] Nature for Wordsworth exhibits a "general tendency"; he speaks of "the tide of things." [3] In nature, "even that which by itself appears impure and confused, still, in its essence, contributes to the glory and divinity of the whole." [4] There is "a spirit and pulse of good" necessarily attached to everything.[5] Prime Nature instinctively works for good. Every-

9. I discuss, below, the relationship of Imagination to reason.
1. "Lines Written in Early Spring," l. 22.
2. *5*, 290.
3. *The Prelude*, II, 385; "The Old Cumberland Beggar," l. 164.
4. Schelling, *4*, 252.
5. "The Old Cumberland Beggar," ll. 77–9.

thing done unconsciously is good, for it is done with an inner necessity which is nothing other than the divine purposiveness expressed in living reality. What Wordsworth said of Toussaint L'Overture and his ideals is, in an analogous sense, true of God's purposes:

> Thou hast left behind
> Powers that will work for thee; air, earth, and skies;
> There's not a breathing of the common wind
> That will forget thee; thou hast great allies.[6]

And nature's goals are necessarily realized, too, in the unconscious functions of "man's unconquerable mind." What is unconscious is instinctive; it moves instinctively toward the good.

> A gracious Spirit o'er this earth presides,
> And o'er the heart of man: invisibly
> It comes, directing those to works of love
> Who care not, know not, think not what they do.[7]

Schelling speaks of a "power by which we, even in our free activity, without our knowledge, and even against our wills, realize goals unawares." [8] That is the reason for nature's harmonious interactions. Unconsciously, the things of nature mutually sustain one another. Note the force of the word "destined" in the following passage (lines 15–21) from "The Old Cumberland Beggar":

> He sat, and ate his food in solitude:
> And ever, scattered from his palsied hand,
> That, still attempting to prevent the waste,
> Was baffled still, the crumbs in little showers
> Fell on the ground; and the small mountain birds,
> Not venturing yet to peck their destined meal,
> Approached within the length of half his staff.

6. "To Toussaint L'Ouverture," ll. 9–12.
7. *The Prelude*, V, 516–19.
8. *3*, 616.

Yet the path of unconscious nature toward the good is not simply and unequivocably necessary. It is, as Hegel would have it, the necessary path of freedom. Man's consciousness is not essentially different from nature; it is simply the highest stage in the "gradual approach to freedom." The freedom in consciousness is simply an enlargement or extension of the autonomy which characterizes all living selfhood. "The essence of the I is freedom," and *Ichheit* characterizes all things; "The I is the only substance." Autonomous selfhood is essential to the life of things. "Life is the autonomy of phenomena. It is the scheme of freedom as it is revealed in Nature." [9] There is freedom everywhere in the throbbing vitality of things. "All beings have their properties which spread Beyond themselves, a power by which they make Some other being conscious of their life." [1] Thus, "It is a beauteous evening, calm, and free." In an undated sonnet, Wordsworth is more explicit on the connection between life and freedom:

> How does the Meadow-flower its bloom unfold?
> Because the lovely little flower is free
> Down to its root, and, in that freedom, bold;
> And so the grandeur of the Forest-tree
> Comes not by casting in a formal mould,
> But from its *own* divine vitality.[2]

Unconscious nature is thus both free and determined. Here as elsewhere, opposites do not exclude one another but are reciprocally unified. The things of nature live their own lives; they freely follow their own instincts, yet, at the same time, they are following "Nature's holy plan."

9. Schelling, *1*, 179, 192, 249.
1. MS lines quoted in Wordsworth, *5*, 286.
2. *"A Poet!* He hath put his heart to school," ll. 9–14.

> Glad Hearts! without reproach or blot;
> Who do thy work and know it not.[3]

By freely living their own lives, things necessarily interact for the mutual good. (The *Fable of the Bees* is given universal validity.) The old beggar eats his bread, and the birds await their destined meal. The village folk give alms freely, to the benefit of everything everywhere, including themselves. This is the course of "general tendency."

But human consciousness and freedom may not fit into the pattern. In man, instinct can become subverted by consciousness.[4] Consciousness may become pure arbitrariness. "This is arbitrariness or consciously free activity."[5] Conscious freedom can break away; it can cut itself off from the reciprocal tide of things. Man can, as Lawrence put it, deny his connections. In him, where freedom is greatest, the very source and sustenance of freedom may be forgotten.

> Spirit that knows no insulated spot,
> No chasm, no solitude; from link to link
> It circulates, the Soul of all the worlds.
> This is the freedom of the universe;
> Unfolded still the more, more visible,
> The more we know; and yet is reverenced least,
> And least respected in the human Mind,
> Its most apparent home.[6]

The human mind can separate itself from the life of the whole. Man has a degree of freedom which is given to nothing else in nature. When this *Willkür* is connected to

3. "Ode to Duty," ll. 13–14.
4. Cf. the original version of "Ode to Duty," *4*, 83:
> All Natures thy behest obey:
> Man only murmurs; he alone
> In wilfulness rejects thy sway.

5. Schelling, *3*, 633.
6. *The Excursion*, IX, 13–20, composed 1798.

the life of things, man continues to participate in general tendency. When it becomes disconnected, man is capable of evil. "Man alone stands at the point of divergence between good and evil. Only in him is the bond which unites the two principles not a necessary one. . . . Evil is not in Nature; it is not animal or subhuman but specifically human and personal." [7]

Evil is specifically human because consciousness is. Consciousness is not in itself evil; it has, in fact, a capacity to attain the highest glory and goodness. But consciousness, of all the elements in nature, is the only thing that can be radically perverted. Consciousness, employed wrongly, "Mis-shapes the beauteous forms of things." [8] Only consciousness has the unhappy capacity to pore on things minute "In disconnection dead and spiritless." [9] That is a perversion of mind. It is

> the very littleness of life.
> Such consciousness I deem but accidents,
> Relapses from the one interior life
> That lives in all things, sacred from the touch
> Of that false secondary power by which
> In weakness we create distinctions.[1]

Schelling makes explicit the point implied by Wordsworth's use of the word "relapse."

> It is not because of their science but because of their *guilt* that such finitude should exist for certain philosophers. Their own will has strayed from the unity. It wants to have a being for itself, and it therefore fails to see either itself or things as they really are, namely, in God. And since, furthermore, the re-

7. Hartmann, *Die Philosophie des deutschen Idealismus, 1,* 170.
8. "The Tables Turned," l. 27.
9. MS lines composed 1797–98, Wordsworth, 5, 402, l. 62.
1. MS lines, *The Prelude,* p. 512.

ligious view is precisely the seeing of all things in God, without any need for proof or further grounding, but simply with a complete innocence of the contrary possibility, such a finite world can only come about by the straying of the individual will from God who is the unity and blessedness of all things. It can only come from a truly Platonic fall, in which state man believes that the dead, absolutely manifold world which he conceives in separation is actually the true and real world. . . . The fact of the existence of such a world in human consciousness is precisely as widespread as the fact of sin. Indeed this is the very fact of sin itself.[2]

The root of all evil is consciousness operating in separation, consciousness denying its connections. This produces not only false knowledge but, as Schelling implied, false action.

The principal milieu of false action is society. Most evil can be traced to that separation which is imposed by artificial institutions. And artificiality is a name for productions of the meddling intellect, of thought in isolation from the whole. When Wordsworth speaks opprobriously of custom, he means artificial or arbitrary custom. He means convention which has become a law unto itself like the isolated intellect which produced it. Such conventions have no connection with nature or with general tendency.

> If such be Nature's holy plan,
> Have I not reason to lament
> What man has made of man? [3]

Once the man-made, arbitrary conventions are there, they exercise a tyrannic influence which is similar, as I shall note, to what Wordsworth conceives to be the tyranny of

2. 7, 81–2.
3. "Lines Written in Early Spring," ll. 22–4.

objects. Custom tyrannizes over the mind, for when we conform to customs produced upon false premises, we know and act falsely. We can no longer see things as they truly are and, therefore, we cannot, like the brave and wise Rob Roy, seek our moral creed "in the principles of things." [4] Arbitrary custom not only separates man from nature, from the tide of things, but, more specifically, by clouding "the great social principle of life," "Society has parted man from man." [5] And even Schelling, who thrived on sophisticated intercourse with urbane artists and philosophers, deplored that "dulness and deadness of the whole spirit which is the inheritance of men corrupted by society. Here the moral sense is diseased." [6] In the same spirit, Wordsworth speaks of

> the fierce confederate storm
> Of sorrow, barricadoed evermore
> Within the walls of cities.[7]

But it would clearly be wrong to accuse Schelling of idyllic Rousseauism, and unjust so to accuse Wordsworth. Wordsworth was no city-bred dreamer of pastorals. Settled again in his valley, he remarks,

> so be it.
> I came not dreaming of unruffled life,
> Untainted manners; born among the hills,
> Bred also there, I wanted not a scale
> To regulate my hopes. Pleased with the good,

---

4. "Rob Roy's Grave," ll. 17–20:
> Say, then, that he was wise as brave;
> As wise in thought as bold in deed:
> For in the principles of things
> *He* sought his moral creed.

5. *The Prelude*, II, 408; XII, 218.
6. 7, 19.
7. Prospectus to *The Recluse*, ll. 78–80.

I shrink not from the evil with disgust,
Or with immoderate pain. I look for Man,
The common Creature of the brotherhood,
Differing but little from the Man elsewhere,
For selfishness, and envy, and revenge,
Ill neighborhood—pity that this should be—
Flattery and double-dealing, strife and wrong.[8]

It is not what cities have made of man but what man has made of man which Wordsworth perceives as evil. The city is simply a symbol of that. In *The Prelude* one of the main points which Wordsworth has to make about London is that even there he finds the tide of things, even there "where the human heart is sick, And the eye feeds it not, and cannot feed." The city symbolizes "the mean and vulgar works of man" and the power of "habit to enslave the mind." [9] But the city is not the exclusive locus of those evils, nor is it in itself exclusively evil.[1] For

8. *The Recluse*, ll. 346–57, 5, 325.
9. *The Prelude*, XII, 202–3; I, 435; XIII, 139.
1. The true antithesis would probably be, even for symbolic purposes, not city vs. country, but men in crowds vs. man alone with nature. But even this antithesis overstates the case. Cf. Plitt, *Aus Schellings Leben*, 2, 310: "Die Einsamkeit erlaubt uns, auch wieder an uns selbst, an unser Liebstes und Bestes zu denken; da finden wir im eigentlichen Verstand unser Inneres wieder und freuen uns, dass es noch da ist." Thus, also, Wordsworth, *The Recluse*, ll. 592–601, 612–19, 5, 333–4:

> Say boldly then that solitude is not
> Where these things are: he truly is alone,
> He of the multitude whose eyes are doomed
> To hold a vacant commerce day by day
> With objects wanting life, repelling love;
> He by the vast Metropolis immured,
> Where pity shrinks from unremitting calls,
> Where numbers overwhelm humanity,
> And neighborhood serves rather to divide
> Than to unite.
>
> Far from the living and dead wilderness
> Of the thronged World, Society is here

evil is "a variety of disease," and disease is to be found wherever man separates himself from nature, whether in city or in country. Wordsworth never denies value to human institutions when they seem natural, which is to say, unarbitrary. Without such institutions, man could never achieve his true purposes.

> oppression worse than death
> Salutes the Being at his birth, where grace
> Of culture hath been utterly unknown.[2]

An entire book of *The Prelude* is devoted to books and to the "great Nature that exists in works of mighty Poets." [3] It is not civilization as such which Wordsworth views as evil, nor is it that which civilization calls evil. If a man be connected with nature, he is good, though he be a rogue. Those lying little gypsies are surely good in Wordsworth's view, and so is old Adam, the thief who, in the middle of London, still retains his connection with things:

> And his bright eyes look brighter,
> set off by the streak
> Of the unfaded rose that still blooms on his
> cheek.[4]

Even human suffering is not seen as evil, so long as the sufferer remains wedded to nature. The suffering is taken up into the goodness of the total process, which is itself beyond merely human good and evil. Everything which truly participates is right. A procession of sufferers passes: Margaret, Ruth, Michael, the old Beggar. Their half-

---

> A true Community, a genuine frame
> Of many into one incorporate.
> *That* must be looked for here, paternal sway,
> One household, under God, for high and low,
> One family and one mansion.

2. *The Prelude*, XII, 194–6.
3. Ibid., V, 618–19.
4. "The Farmer of Tilsbury Vale," ll. 7–8.

conscious sense of participation makes them uncomplaining. They move in the tide of necessary goodness.

Yet, it is not for them to experience the "Sorrow that is not sorrow, but delight." [5] That experience is reserved for the mind in its highest potency, for the mind which is *aware* of the pulse of good which is linked to every mode of being. After *The Ruined Cottage,* in the manuscript version, Wordsworth appends some lines which spell out the meaning of Margaret's tragedy.

> I know not how
> But to some eye within me all appeared
> Colours and forms of a strange discipline.
> The trouble which they sent into my thought
> Was sweet.[6]

In Imagination, man becomes aware of the necessary bond in nature between evil and goodness:

> And many a legend peopling the dark woods
> Nourished Imagination in her growth,
> And gave the mind that apprehensive power
> By which she is made quick to recognize
> The moral properties and scope of things.[7]

Nature's implicit moral teleology has become aware of itself.

But Imagination also enlarges goodness. It continues goodness on a new level. I have defined Imagination as a reciprocal unity of active and passive functions. In the ethical dimension this means a unity of freedom and necessity, and in Imagination such a unity is consciously attained. Schelling calls it "the identity of the conscious and the unconscious within the I, and the consciousness of that

---

5. *The Prelude,* XII, 245.
6. MS lines, 5, 400.
7. *The Ruined Cottage,* ll. 169–73, 5, 383.

identity." Imagination becomes aware of its own unin-
tended goodness.

> Freedom is to be necessity; necessity freedom. Now,
> in contrast to freedom, necessity is nothing other than
> the unconscious. What is unconscious in me is un-
> arbitrary. That which is conscious in me is freely
> willed. To say that freedom shall again be necessary
> means that through freedom, by means of free action,
> something shall arise unconsciously and without my
> intercession—something I did not intend. To express
> this in another way: conscious or free activity . . .
> shall stand over against an unconscious activity. When
> this is the case, even in the most uninhibited expres-
> sions of freedom there will arise something unarbitrary,
> something, perhaps, even contrary to that which is
> willed. And this unarbitrary realization will be some-
> thing which the conscious will, by itself, could never
> accomplish.[8]

That is Wordsworth's wise passiveness. It is an active
passivity. *"We* can feed this mind of ours, In a wise passiveness." The "impulse from a vernal wood" tells us of evil
and good because the impulse comes from the mind as
well as from the wood, as the language itself suggests.[9]
The free activity of the mind is unified with that which the
mind passively receives. "Consciousness transcends the innocence [of nature] and therefore requires a direct reconciliation and freely willed submission, in which freedom
comes forth from the battle at once victor and vanquished.
This conscious reconciliation, which takes the place of
the unconscious identity with Nature . . . reinstates the
unity on a higher level."[1]

But how can wise passiveness, as such, ever realize good-

8. *3*, 612, 594.
9. "Expostulation and Reply," ll. 23-4; "The Tables Turned," ll. 21-4.
Italics mine.
1. Schelling, *5*, 290.

ness in the realm of ethical action? What is the compulsive principle which makes us carry out that which we know to be right? "For what I would, that do I not; but what I hate, that do I." St. Paul could say that, but Wordsworth and Schelling cannot. Enthusiasm denies the implications in the doctrine of original sin. ("Trailing clouds of glory do we come.") Enthusiasm sees no tension between knowledge and action. The activity of wise passiveness joins what is ethically desirable to that which is actually desired. What is desired in knowledge is also desired in will.

> Yet not the less would I throughout
> Still act according to the voice
> Of my own wish; and feel past doubt
> That my submissiveness was choice.[2]

For Wordsworth and Schelling, as for Socrates, to know the good is to be good. The problem of ethics is solved when we come to know the principles of things.

> Thus deeply drinking-in the soul of things,
> We shall be wise perforce; and, while inspired
> By choice, and conscious that the Will is free,
> Shall move unswerving, even as if impelled
> By strict necessity, along the path
> Of order and of good.[3]

An irresistible power for good overcomes man when he becomes a conscious part of nature's life. Schelling speaks of "that underlying identity of the theoretical and the practical [i.e. actively ethical] in us. Only by means of this do our affections become thoughts, and our thoughts affections. Only by virtue of this does the real become ideal, and the ideal real." [4]

2. "Ode to Duty," ll. 41–4.
3. *The Excursion,* IV, 1265–70, composed 1797–98.
4. *I,* 413.

For this reason revelation is redemption and redemption is revelation, a point which I have touched on in the third chapter. Revelation can be described as man's conscious, imaginative knowledge of his participation in nature. The denial of such participation is only possible in thought, not in being. Evil is an aberration which springs from false knowledge, from the freedom to be isolated, to see chimeras, and to misunderstand. "There is no breaking away in fact; there is only separation in thought. By false Imagination, thought produces . . . isolated existences." [5] Thus, the redemption from evil lies constantly at hand. By true Imagination, consciousness can discover its own error and return to truth. In their deepest essence *all* men are part of the whole. Redemption can be learned. The day "of joy in widest commonalty spread" is at hand:

> Why is this glorious Creature to be found
> One only in ten thousand? What one is,
> Why may not many be? What bars are thrown
> By Nature in the way of such a hope? [6]

"The Rebirth," says Schelling, "will necessarily begin when the divinity of Nature and the great unity of all being are again comprehended." [7]

>   for there's not a man
> That lives who hath not had his godlike hours,
> And knows not what majestic sway we have,
> As natural beings in the strength of nature. [8]

Imagination realizes the goals of life in yet another realm. In the productions of art, it continues creation. If the conscious realization of implicit goodness is the ethical

5. Fuhrmans, p. 72.
6. *The Prelude*, XII, 90–3.
7. 2, 73. Quoted in Fuhrmans, p. 40.
8. *The Prelude*, III, 191–4.

goal, then the conscious realization of implicit beauty is the aesthetic goal. Art is nature's self-affirmation as self-glorification and self-creation. Creative power, like freedom, characterizes everything in nature, and, like freedom, it finds its highest, most conscious expression in man. Neither Wordsworth nor Schelling forgets that man's artistic power is an extension of the creative force which transfuses all of nature. Human art *grows* out of nature as Wordsworth's chapels, houses, and cottages seem to grow out of the earth, continuations of the one life.

> Ye might think
> That it had sprung self-raised from earth, or grown
> Out of the living rock, to be adorned
> By nature only; but if thither led,
> Ye would discover, then, a studious work
> Of many fancies.[9]

Schelling speaks of "the bird intoxicated by music who surpasses himself in soulful notes, and the little, artistically gifted creature who, without practice or instruction, accomplishes simple architectural works." Art crowns the productivity of the cosmos, yet it is simply a higher, more conscious development of that productivity. "One notes a continual progression from simple matter up to organization (where productive Nature unconsciously returns upon itself) and from there, by agency of Reason and *Willkür*, up to the highest union of freedom and necessity. This is art, where productive Nature consciously comprehends and completes itself." Thus, "there is an unbroken series from the simplest element of Nature up to the highest and most comprehensive: the work of art." "My general view of art," says Schelling, "is that it constitutes an efflux from the Absolute." [1]

---

9. *The Excursion*, VI, 1143–8, composed 1800.
1. 7, 300; 3, 634; 4, 89; 5, 372. A translation of Schelling's entire lecture

Life's creative power is reciprocity seen as transformation. Life transforms elements by bringing them together in dynamic wholes. Transformation is interfusion. Wordsworth is speaking of a chapel:

> It seemed—wall, window, roof and tower—
> To bow to some transforming power,
> And blend with the surrounding trees.[2]

In the final book of *The Prelude,* Wordsworth relates how a mountain mist seemed to transform a far-reaching range of hills into a vast ocean. In the midst of this ocean

> Was a blue chasm; a fracture in the vapour,
> A deep and gloomy breathing-place through which
> Mounted the roar of waters, torrents, streams
> Innumerable, roaring with one voice.
> The universal spectacle throughout
> Was shaped for admiration and delight,
> Grand in itself alone, but in that breach
> Through which the homeless voice of waters rose,
> That dark deep thoroughfare had Nature lodg'd
> The Soul, the Imagination of the whole.[3]

Schelling is not less conscious of this "analogy betwixt The mind of man and nature": [4]

> As the sun stands free in the firmament, binding and unifying all in the force of its bright light, so stands the *Gemüt* of eternal Nature within the unified life itself, as its unity and, so to speak, its divine Imagination. It stands free and autonomous as the source of

---

"Concerning the Relation of the Plastic Arts to Nature" is to be found in Herbert Read, *The True Voice of Feeling* (New York, Pantheon, 1953), pp. 323–64.

2. *Peter Bell,* ll. 858–60.
3. *The Prelude,* XIII, 56–65.
4. MS lines, *The Prelude,* p. 600.

all feeling existence. It is the heartbeat of visible Nature, moving everything in her holy body. It is the
source of every movement and impulse, and of the inwardness in all creation.[5]

The imagination of the whole is like man's Imagination.
The latter is but a reflection or extension of the former.
The vital power in man allows him to effect "Like transformations" by a like process, namely that of active reciprocity. Here, the conscious, active mind is one element,
and that which the mind receives is the other. It is always
through the interaction of these two that man transforms
"the outward face of things." [6] There is always mind
and thing. Thinghood as such is never absent. Wordsworth
speaks of

> the mind,
> And of the power she has within herself
> To ennoble all things.[7]

Such reciprocity is not a rare or special occurrence. The
power is there from the beginning; it is something natural,
instinctive, fundamental. Even the infant babe performs
such a function. It is the basic character of mind.

> From nature largely he receives; nor so
> Is satisfied, but largely gives again,
>
> . . . . .
>
> Even as an agent of the one great mind,
> Creates, creator and receiver both,
> Working but in alliance with the works
> Which it beholds.—Such, verily, is the first
> Poetic spirit of our human life.[8]

5. 7, 202.
6. *The Prelude*, XIII, 94, 78.
7. MS lines, 5, 318.
8. *The Prelude*, II, 267-76.

That is Schelling's basic view of mind. The very first vital, dialectical interaction with nature exhibits the same principle as the higher functions of the mind. More advanced functions are simply the life of consciousness in a "higher potency." "The poetic faculty is, in its first potency, original perception. Conversely, it is simply productive perception repeating itself in its highest potency which we call the poetic faculty. One and the same function characterizes both." And, like all the stages of consciousness, the highest stage, artistic Imagination, "is based on the identity of conscious and unconscious activity." [9]

Yet, even though the stages be essentially the same, they are to be distinguished. The true artist extends creation because he has become *aware* of the

> mighty world
> Of eye, and ear,—both what they half create,
> And what perceive.[1]

Artistic productivity "reproduces with consciousness and freedom what unconscious intelligence had produced unconsciously and necessarily." [2] This awareness is the distinctive feature of art. It is given to chosen souls. Wordsworth's poet has

> a peculiar dower, a sense
> By which he is enabled to perceive
> Something unseen before.[3]

Schelling uses the word "Genius." In his productions, the Genius reveals the "unborn beauty" of things.[4] But his

---

9. Schelling, *3*, 626; *5*, 384.
1. "Tintern Abbey," ll. 105–7.
2. Hartmann, p. 142.
3. *The Prelude*, XII, 303–5.
4. *5*, 345: "Ich rede von einer heiligeren Kunst, derjenigen, welche, nach den Ausdrücken der Alten, ein Werkzeug der Götter, eine Verkündigerin göttliche Geheimnisse, die Enthüllerin der Ideen ist, von

awareness and creativity operates within the reciprocity which characterizes all of nature's transformations. The power of genius is not something radically new; it comes directly from his knowledge. Knowing compels doing in the case of artistic creation, just as it does in the realm of ethical action. "It is as if in rare and unusual men, artists in the highest sense of the word, the unchanging identity upon which all existence is founded lays aside the veil with which, in other men, it surrounds itself, and becomes directly affected by things. And it is as if, in return, it exerts a direct effect upon things." The "unborn beauty" or the "something unseen before" is implicit in things, as the oak tree is implicit in the acorn. The creativity of genius is conscious explicitation, and this results from conscious reciprocity. As in the good man, the freedom of the genius is necessity; his submissiveness is choice, and vice versa.

> Those rules which genius can throw aside are those which a merely mechanical Understanding prescribes. Genius is autonomous. It shuns only external laws, not its own, for it is genius only insofar as it is the highest lawfulness. Philosophy recognizes this lawfulness. For philosophy is not only autonomous but also advances toward the principle of all autonomy. In every period, therefore, we observe that the true artists are silent, simple, great and necessary in their manner —like Nature.[5]

This pronouncement could stand as a paraphrase of Wordsworth's sonnet, *"A Poet!—He hath put his heart to school."*

---

der ungebornen Schönheit, deren unentweihter Strahl nur reine Seelen inwohnend erleuchtet, und deren Gestalt dem sinnlichen Auge ebenso verborgen und unzugänglich ist als die der gleichen Wahrheit."

5. Schelling, *3*, 616; *5*, 349.

Because true art is a conscious enlargement of the beauty and creativity in nature, as it were, a growth out of nature, it has an honored place in the commonwealth of things. Its fundamental character is explicitation and realization. Art makes real and explicit what might remain potential and implicit. It is a completion in nature's vital growth from and to God. Art and natural objects are both "products of one and the same activity." In art, as in knowledge, life becomes aware of itself, and, as in ethical action, life realizes itself. Because art is partially a product of consciousness, it is available to consciousness. Like philosophy, it is an articulate instrument of revelation. "Through art, the rapt student of Nature learns how to recognize the true *Urbilder,* which, in Nature, are half hidden." [6] The finite product, art, always expresses the *Urbild* of infinite life. It consciously finds this infinite in all its objects. That is the mind's peculiar contribution in "spousal verse." The mind adds the aura of infinitude, "whence our dignity originates."

> I remember well
> That in life's every-day appearances
> I seem'd about this period to have sight
> Of a new world, a world, too, that was fit
> To be transmitted and made visible
> To other eyes, as having for its base
> That whence our dignity originates,
> That which both gives it being and maintains
> A balance, an ennobling interchange
> Of action from within and from without,
> The excellence, pure spirit, and best power
> Both of the object seen, and eye that sees.[7]

Art realizes the underlying life of all things by making ex-

6. Ibid., 3, 626; 5, 351–2.
7. *The Prelude*, XII, 368–79.

plicit the "new world" which lies implicitly around us. Art is truth and glory. In "life's every-day appearances" it reveals the unborn beauty. It is not only a product of the divine life but an expression of it. Like nature, it is at once product and productivity. Wordsworth hopes,

> that a work of mine,
> Proceeding from the depth of untaught things,
> Enduring and creative, might become
> A power like one of Nature's.[8]

It is not mere rhetoric when Wordsworth attributes to poetry a living power like that in the "motions of the winds." For poetry is that selfsame power in a higher potency:

> Visionary Power
> Attends upon the motions of the winds
> Embodied in the mystery of words.
> There darkness makes abode, and all the host
> Of shadowy things do work their changes there,
> As in a mansion like their proper home;
> Even forms and substances are circumfused
> By that transparent veil with light divine;
> And through the turnings intricate of Verse,
> Present themselves as objects recognis'd,
> In flashes, and with a glory scarce their own.[9]

It is not irrelevant to the true character of his poetry that Wordsworth should have said, "I wish either to be considered as a Teacher, or as nothing." [1] Wordsworth's most highly regarded poetry is not didactic in the ordinary meaning of the word, but it is didactic in the sense that it

8. Ibid., XII, 309–12.

9. Ibid., V, 619–29.

1. *The Letters of William and Dorothy Wordsworth*, ed. Ernest de Selincourt, *The Middle Years*, Vol. *1* (London, Oxford Univ. Press, 1937), p. 170: to Sir George Beaumont, 1808.

is philosophical, prophetic, and apocalyptic. The time of universal glory is at hand, the time of "joy in widest commonalty spread." Schelling, too, announces the immanent rebirth which attends man's return to nature. Implicit in every poem is the admonition to look and to see. This implicit admonition is didactic because to see means to see the implicit life and goodness of all things.

> All things shall speak of Man, and we shall read
> Our duties in all forms.[2]

The didactic element is not accidental but essential. Wordsworth's poetry is necessarily ethical and philosophic. For the kind of beauty he sees and creates is inseparable from goodness and truth. Imaginative poetry is connected with all the teleologies of life; it belongs to the "tide of things." Wordsworth does not exhort; he explicitates nature's exhortation. It is nature which exhorts us to see, to feel, to be, and to affirm. Behind all lies the question which states the goal of poetic striving:

> is there not
> An art, a music, and a strain of words
> That shall be life, the acknowledged voice of life?[3]

Up to this point I have discussed the teleologies of Imagination primarily from the cosmological point of view, because I consider an understanding of Imagination's cosmic character to be essential to an understanding of its psychological character. It is in relation to these larger issues that the psychological aspects begin to have a meaning. Inevitably, one must speak of faculties. For Enthusiasm, there are, fundamentally, three kinds of mental faculties: active ones, passive ones, and faculties which unite those two. But to speak of mental faculties is to

2. MS lines, 5, 401.
3. *The Recluse*, ll. 401–3, 5, 327.

hypostatize mental possibilities. A faculty is the possibility of a function. It is convenient to hypostatize in this fashion. Following a long tradition, both Wordsworth and Schelling give mental possibilities a name, and I follow their practice in my analysis. But it is important to remember that function and not faculty is the real object of inquiry. It is what the mind does, and not the nature of its possibility for doing it, that primarily interests Wordsworth and Schelling.

On the one hand, there are faculties which name the free and active functions of the mind, faculties like "intellect," "will," "fancy," "reflection," "understanding." On the other hand, the mind exhibits a purely passive function which is not free, nor willed, nor conscious in the same way as the other faculties. This function is primarily "sense perception," "sensible intuition," or *"sinnliche Anschauung."* Here the basic characteristic of the function is that it cannot be freely altered. It is nonarbitrary; it relates to necessity and the unconscious. Thirdly, we have those functions which are forms of Imagination (and conversely, Imagination can be thought of as forms of them): "instinct," "emotion," "intellectual perception," "reason."

The active, arbitrary functions of the mind are necessary to Imagination, and both Wordsworth and Schelling value them highly. This is especially true in the case of artistic creation.

> This *efficacious* spirit chiefly lurks
> Among those passages of life in which
> We have had deepest feeling that the mind
> Is lord and master, and that outward sense
> Is but the obedient servant of her will.

Wordsworth praises that "independent world Created out of pure Intelligence." [4] For without this plastic and some-

4. *The Prelude,* XI, 269–73. Italics mine. VI, 186–7.

times rebellious power, the mind could not bestow new splendor on the setting sun. There could be no imaginative art. This independent power, as such, is what Wordsworth sometimes calls fancy. Fancy is no more Imagination than understanding is reason. The independent function is simply necessary to the higher, more inclusive function. "Understanding is also reason [fancy is also Imagination] and nothing else; only it is reason in its non-totality. It is just as necessarily and eternally with reason as the temporal always accompanies the eternal. Understanding has no real life of its own, but only through reason." Schelling compares, in similar fashion, *Phantasie* to *Einbildungskraft*. The passage seems elliptic but its general sense is, I think, clear: "In relation to fancy, I define Imagination as that faculty which conceives and forms the productions of art. Fancy perceives art in an external fashion. It has to do with that which art, so to speak, casts out from itself, and externally displays." [5]

Fancy and understanding are valued as components of more inclusive functions. But what they produce in and for themselves becomes "blind vacancy" which is "scooped out By help of dreams." [6] Imagination is always controlled by something nonarbitrary; fancy or understanding alone are purely arbitrary and "vacant." "Imagination . . . is the faculty of Ideas. It is that which we call theoretical reason. Reason is to be distinguished from *Schwärmerei* in this: that the one is Imagination within the bounds of the moral postulate, the other is unbridled *Phantasie*. The one gives birth to Ideas, the other to chimeras." Mere fancy and the mere meddling intellect represent a retreat into *isolated* subjectivity. For that reason they produce, by themselves, falsehood and alienation. The exclusive functioning of either separates man from the one life. Under-

5. 7, 42; 5, 395.
6. Prospectus to *The Recluse*, ll. 37–8.

standing "wants to consider as separated that which is eternally and absolutely posited as one. To that which has reality only in unity, it wants to give a reality independent of the unity." [7] The danger of all the active faculties is that they can feed upon themselves autonomously. When they do not function with "blended might," they succeed only in separating the mind from real truth, goodness, and beauty.

> I seemed to learn
> That what we see of forms and images
> Which float along our minds, and what we feel
> Of active or recognizable thought,
> Prospectiveness, or intellect, or will,
> Not only is not worthy to be deemed
> Our being, to be prized as what we are,
> But is the very littleness of life.

Such pure "vacancy" is actively deleterious in relation to the moral dimension. Wordsworth speaks of,

> that abasement into which perforce
> The mind must sink that hangs on its own works
> With an exclusive dotage. [8]

Schelling states the issue passionately and clearly:

> Pure reflection is a spiritual sickness in man, all the more so where it tyrannizes the whole man. It destroys his higher existence in the bud, and kills in the root his spiritual life, which can only proceed from unity. It is an evil which follows man through life, and destroys his ability to perceive truly even common objects. But the dissecting activity of reflection is not limited to the world of appearances. In separating this world from the spiritual principle, it fills the mental

7. Schelling, *1*, 431; 7, 151.
8. MS lines, *The Prelude*, pp. 512, 593.

world with chimeras. Against these chimeras no war
is possible, for they lie beyond all reason. Pure reflection makes man's separation from the world permanent, for it looks upon the latter as a thing in itself,
which neither perception nor Imagination, understanding nor reason is able to reach.[9]

There is, however, something which *can* redeem the
mind from its exclusive dotage and bring it into reciprocity with the divine whole:

> Hail to the visible Presence, hail to thee
> Delightful Valley, habitation fair!
> And to whatever else of outward form
> Can give us inward help, can purify,
> And elevate and harmonise.[1]

External nature lies before us to steal us from our dreams
of blind vacancy and unite us with the world. "All healing
lies only in nature. She alone is the true antidote to abstraction." "Nature is the only dam against the arbitrariness of thought and the freedom of abstraction." Nature
redeems the mind from its isolation. We can only begin
to *see* nature when our minds begin to relinquish their
exclusive mastery. "To the degree that we silence ourselves
in ourselves, so speaks she to us." [2]

But there is also danger from the other side. As Wordsworth phrased it, there may be "a subjugation of an oppo-
site character." The mind can be controlled exclusively
by its object. Characteristically, for this event, Wordsworth
employs the metaphor of slavery:

> By objects of the senses not enslaved.

> The tendency, too potent in itself,

9. 2, 13–14.
1. *The Recluse*, ll. 299–303, 5, 324.
2. Schelling, 7, 19, 36; 2, 378.

Of habit to enslave the mind, I mean
Oppress it by the laws of vulgar sense.[3]

The tyranny of objects can produce the same kind of isolation and lifelessness that blind vacancy produces. The two
are, in fact, corollaries. To hang upon an object in brute
slavery is to see it as isolated from the living whole which
only Imagination can know. And, to think about objects
abstractly is to think of them as isolated. Both one-sided
sense perception and one-sided mental activity have separated, finite objects. "It is the fault of the individual that
a mere finite thing should exist for him." [4] That was Peter
Bell's fault. Neglectful of the universal life, he was a mere
thinker and a mere perceiver.

A primrose by a river's brim
A yellow primrose was to him,
And it was nothing more.

Peter Bell's failure to see is connected with his failure to
feel.

The soft blue sky did never melt
Into his heart.

Peter's heart was deficient. His redemption comes when he,
at last, begins to feel.

And now is Peter taught to feel
That man's heart is a holy thing;
And Nature, through a world of death,
Breathes into him a second breath,
More searching than the breath of spring.[5]

The nature of Peter's feelings is important, so important
that I have reserved my discussion of it for the end of this

3. MS lines, *The Prelude*, p. 524; *The Prelude*, XIII, 138–40.
4. Schelling, 7, 82.
5. *Peter Bell*, ll. 248–50, 263–4, 1071–5.

chapter. Here, I am concerned to point out the abstract fact that emotion as such effects an unconscious unity of man and the world. Man's emotions and, in related fashion, his unconscious instincts constitute the first stage of Imagination. Emotion is the most basic element in the mind, and it

> reconciles
> Discordant elements and makes them move
> In one society.[6]

Schelling calls this basic element *Gemüt,* and thus emphasizes its two-sided nature. Gemüt connotes both activity and passivity, thinking and feeling. It is semiconscious and semiaffective. As we have already noted, Gemüt is a principle both in nature and in man, a point of identity in both: "When we look at things and do not perceive the essence within them but only the empty, abstract form, then they say nothing to our inner being. We must apply our own spirit, our own Gemüt to them, that they shall answer us." [7] Nonreflective feeling has an honorific status for Wordsworth because feeling marks our connection with the inwardness of creation. The infant is no outcast; "feeling has to him imparted strength." [8] The emotions are at once conscious and unconscious. They are instinctive. When we feel, we are aware of emotion; but we do not control it. "Feeling can never betray," said Schleiermacher, "for there being and consciousness [*Sein und Bewusstsein*] are the same." [9] Garrod's remarks about Wordsworth are, in this case, surely correct: "The path from sense to im-

6. *The Prelude,* I, 353–5.
7. 7, 294.
8. *The Prelude,* II, 269.
9. Cited by Paul Kluckhohn, *Das Ideengut der deutschen Romantik* (Tübingen, Niemeyer, 1953), p. 44.

agination does not pass through the intellect. It passes through the affections." [1] Feeling guarantees our connection with the life of things. Wordsworth speaks of

> Emotion which best foresight need not fear
> Most worthy then of trust when most intense.[2]

There is always an element of emotion in Imagination, but emotion, as such, is only the first stage of Imagination. Just as the cosmos exhibits a gradual and progressive growth, so does the mind. In fact, the development of the two is analogous. "The external world lies spread out before us, that we may find again in it, the history of our spirit." [3] The teleology of the cosmos is expressed in the teleology of the individual mind. For Wordsworth this development begins with the "unconscious" feelings of childhood and culminates in the poetic or philosophic mind. Yet, the final stage is not cut off from the emotions which started the development on its true path. The final stage is "feeling intellect." There is emotion both in the present, higher experience of nature and also in the remembrance of past emotion. But the emotion is different in the final stage; it is mediated by consciousness and knowledge. It is less direct and intense but more constant. It is emotion along with awareness of emotion. This stage comprehends both the "thing Contemplated" and "the Mind and Man Contemplating." [4] As in all organic development, Imagination advances and yet remains the same.

Bateson rightly implies that this is a principal theme of *The Prelude*: "Indeed [Wordsworth's] education in Natural Piety, if we may trust the description of the process in

1. H. W. Garrod, *Wordsworth: Lectures and Essays* (London, Oxford Univ. Press, 1927), p. 144.
2. *The Prelude*, XIII, 115–16.
3. Schelling, *1*, 383.
4. Prospectus to *The Recluse*, ll. 94–6.

The Prelude, seems to have been essentially towards an ever greater consciousness of the feelings the natural scene aroused in him, and a more and more sophisticated appreciation of the causes of those feelings." [5] The idea, "emotion recollected in tranquillity," implies emotion which is mediated by consciousness and self-awareness. In tranquillity, one remembers the emotion, that which caused it, the man who had it, and one perceives the relations of all these to the life of things. This theme is common to Wordsworth and Schelling and to Hegel as well. Apperception is the "truth" of perception, but it does not exclude perception. The earlier stages of mind are not cancelled out in the higher. They are retained and also transcended within a new unity. Were they not retained, the new unity would lose its right to be considered truth. That is the primary meaning of Hegel's "concrete universal." The mind progresses, but it keeps its bearings through its original connection with life.[6]

Yet, the essential fact about mind is that it does advance. "Mind is nothing else than an eternal becoming. Because of this, we can understand a priori the advancing, progres-

---

5. F. W. Bateson, *Wordsworth, A Re-interpretation* (London, Longmans, 1954), pp. 58–9.

6. Richard Kroner, *Hegel's Early Theological Writings* (Chicago, Univ. of Chicago Press, 1948), pp. 19–20: "What was certain in him was his ideal. But the task implied in this ideal—of reconciling life and thought, faith and reason, spirit and intellect, and of expressing the ideal in the form of reflection—was not yet discharged. To this task the years from 1800 to 1807 are dedicated. In the philosophical language of these years, the opposition between life and thought appears in the form of an opposition between intuition and reflection. Is there any possibility of unification? Is there an intuition which can be cast in reflective terms— a reflection which spontaneously returns to intuition? In other words, is there an intuitive reflection or a reflective intuition? An intellectual power equal to the spirit? The final answer is affirmative. Within the intellect itself there is such a power; Hegel calls it 'reason.' Reason leads the intellect to ever higher levels of insight—up to the highest stage of reconciliation."

sive character of our knowledge—from dead matter up to
the idea of a living Nature." That is what Schelling means
when he asserts that "the system of nature is also the system of our spirit." Mind, like nature, is a development toward awareness of nature and, therefore, of itself. It is a
"wrestling of the spirit toward the perception of the underlying, fundamental Nature." [7] Thus, Wordsworth could
say, "Fair seed-time had my soul." In the retrospective
comments in the final book of *The Prelude*, Wordsworth
notes explicitly the character of his mind's development:

> we have traced the stream
> From darkness, and the very place of birth
> In its blind cavern, whence is faintly heard
> The sound of waters; follow'd it to light
> And open day.

As one would expect from the nature of Imagination's
cosmic goals, the psychological goal is also truth and awareness. In relation to this goal, Imagination is reason:

> clearest insight, amplitude of mind,
> And reason in her most exalted mood. [8]

Reason, for Schelling, is but another potency of original
perception, just as is the artistic Imagination. It also joins
the real and ideal worlds, for it belongs to both worlds,
like emotion and Intellectual Perception. "Reason belongs
neither to the real nor to the ideal world exclusively." [9]
Reason's growth is gradual self-awareness. Childhood's
emotional intuition of truth becomes conscious of itself
and, therefore, of the underlying unity and selfhood in all
things:

7. *1*, 367; *2*, 39; *5*, 326.
8. *The Prelude*, XIII, 172–6, 169–70.
9. *5*, 379–80.

    turning the mind in upon itself, [I]
Pored, watch'd, expected, listen'd; spread my thoughts
And spread them with a wider creeping; felt
Incumbencies more awful, visitings
Of the Upholder of the tranquil Soul,
Which underneath all passion lives secure
A steadfast life. But peace! it is enough
To notice that I was ascending now
To such community with highest truth.[1]

That is what Schelling means (he does not imply subjective idealism) when he says, "Intelligence will end in a complete recognition of the identity expressed in the product [*natura naturata*] as an identity whose principle lies in itself [*natura naturans*]. That is to say, intelligence will end in complete self-perception." The final stage is reached when man in full awareness, "and through his own efforts, returns to that condition in which he, unaware of himself, experienced the childhood of his reason." [2] Wordsworth likens the process to the path of a traveler who walks through a mist-covered dell:

           The inward frame
Though slowly opening, opens every day
With process not unlike to that which chears
A pensive Stranger, journeying at his leisure
Through some Helvetian dell, when low-hung mists
Break up, and are beginning to recede;
How pleased he is where thin and thinner grows
The veil, or where it parts at once, to spy
The dark pines thrusting forth their spiky heads;
To watch the spreading lawns with cattle grazed,
Then to be greeted by the scattered huts,
As they shine out; and *see* the streams whose murmur

1. *The Prelude*, III, 112–20.
2. *3*, 615; *2*, 13.

Had soothed his ear while they were hidden: how pleased
To have about him, which way e'er he goes,
Something on every side concealed from view,
In every quarter something visible,
Half-seen or wholly, lost and found again,
Alternate progress and impediment,
And yet a growing prospect in the main.[3]

As I have noted, knowledge is also power. The growth
of knowledge is also the growth of power, for truth is nothing other than life become conscious of itself. The mind
and nature reinforce one another. Their power is "blended
might." "The pure force of things flows together with the
force of our spirit, and both become one outpouring." [4]

> whate'er
> I saw, or heard, or felt, was but a stream
> That flow'd into a kindred stream.[5]

The power of Imagination is that of synthesizing and expressing this intercourse. The mind "strives to represent
the absolute synthesis." [6] That toward which Imagination
strives is explicitation, for the primary synthesis was given
from the very beginning.

> even then,
> A Child, I held unconscious intercourse
> With the eternal Beauty.[7]

But the primary synthesis must be fully expressed, and it
must be communicated. That is the duty of chosen souls.

> I would impart it, I would spread it wide,
> Immortal in the world which is to come.[8]

3. *The Recluse*, ll. 472–90, 5, 329.
4. Schelling, 7, 299.
5. *The Prelude*, VI, 672–4.
6. Schelling, 3, 487.
7. *The Prelude*, I, 588–90.
8. *The Recluse*, ll. 690–1, 5, 336.

The work of art becomes a momentary fulfillment in the constant striving of the imaginative life.

I have said that the emotions are the basic point of contact between mind and nature, the conscious and the unconscious. Feeling is "blended might" on its most fundamental level. Emotion is, in fact, the most basic sanction for Enthusiasm's experience. Emotion, the basic element in Imagination, sanctions Imagination itself. For emotion is the *direct* experience of life. All other levels of Imagination are mediated, developed, explicitated. Emotion is direct, apodictic. There is no greater authority.

To say that emotion is the direct experience of life is to speak of a particular sort of emotion, one which both "feels" and "knows." To see life in stones means to feel their life or link them to some feeling. One feels the inner being of that which is presented as having only an outside. Nature begins to live for Peter Bell when he begins to feel the "blue sky melt into his heart." Only feeling can identify my life, my inwardness with the inwardness of things. "We must apply our own Gemüt to things, that they shall answer us."

> his spirit drank
> The spectacle. Sensation, soul and form
> All melted into him. They swallowed up
> His animal being; in them did he live
> And by them did he live. They were his life.[9]

The sensation which Wordsworth describes by the metaphor "melting" is the emotion of love or, as Scheler would call it, cosmic love. Cosmic love is the spiritual correlate of cosmic life. The clouds, the sky, the hills, the face of "this beauteous world" are alive to us only because we love them; we feel their inner identity with ourselves.

9. *The Ruined Cottage,* ll. 129–33, 5, 382.

Those fields, those hills—what could they less? had laid
Strong hold on his affections, were to him
A pleasurable feeling of blind love,
The pleasure which there is in life itself.[1]

"Nature is not limited to the external, spirit is not limited to the internal. Outside of us there rules the same spirit, and inside of us the same nature." [2] But only feeling-with can make us know that fact. Only cosmic sympathy can provide

> That sense of dim similitude which links
> Our mortal feelings with external forms.[3]

It is this kind of love which Schelling means when he, throughout his early works, uses the word *Band*. The *Band* explains all. It is "the living copula." By it we come to know the life of things:

> Our aim is to know and to recognize the life of matter and every part thereof. But this knowledge is not something which you can grasp in thought. On the contrary, it is from abstract thought that you are to be redeemed. You are to re-enter the basic simplicity of being and sense. Sense is itself nothing but the direct and, as it were, magical feeling of inwardness and affirmation. And, at the same time, it is the *bond* of your own essence with this inwardness and affirmation. Neither the life of nature nor your own deepest meaning is closed off. Rather, it is your own inward death of mind and heart which closes these off to you. It is impossible truly to perceive livingness by a clumsy or arrogant wayfaring over things. For that perception

1. "Michael," ll. 74–7.
2. Hartmann, p. 132.
3. MS lines, *The Prelude*, p. 564.

you must sense the inner love and kinship between
your own spirit and the livingness of nature.[4]

Cosmic love means loving the cosmos and being loved
by it. Man says yes to the world, and the world answers in
kind. There is a "living copula between affirming and being affirmed." [5] This double-sidedness in the relationship
of love accounts for the characteristic confusions in Wordsworth's descriptions of nature. Natural objects seem to
return the poet's own attitude to them. He senses, for example,

> The admiration and the love, the life
> In common things.[6]

Love is the fundamental emotion. The ubiquitous reciprocity of all things is grounded in that basic reciprocity.
The structure of life is nothing other than the structure of
love. Life is at once autonomous and reciprocal activity,
and this is the case because by means of love the life in
things also becomes the life through things. The relationship of love, as it is found in Enthusiasm, is a dialectical
unity of selfhood and otherness. It is an identification of
the self with its object, within the sense of separation and
otherness. Otherness is joined with selfhood, yet neither
is relinquished. As soon as one pole vanishes into its other,
we no longer have enthusiastic love but perfect fusion and
perfect stasis. There is no longer life and temporality but
death.

Love is creative. Where before there were distinct oppositions, now there is unity. Love's transformation is the
type and symbol for all the transformations of Imagination.
"The bond is the living unification of the one and the

4. 2, 374; 7, 61–2.
5. 7, 224.
6. *The Prelude*, I, 117–18.

many. And, along with the bond, there is also that which has, out of unity and multiplicity, become one." [7] The transformations are actualized by the act of love. The paradoxes are real, and true art is nothing other than an expression of transformed reality. It is, ultimately, a product of love.

The direct feeling of cosmic love assures all the paradoxes of reciprocity, yet it is not a mere feeling. It is not a purely blind reaction to things, even in its earliest stages. Enthusiastic love is, essentially, religious faith. The sense of life in myself and in things, my love of the world and its love for me are all connected with my commitment to something absolute and infinite. Cosmic love is, implicitly, a special sort of religion. Schelling expresses it so: "By this image of God's love to Himself (the most beautiful conception of the Subject-Objectification), there is represented at once the birth of the universe out of God and His relationship to it." Love is "the eternal bond of God's self-revelation, by which the infinite is resolved into the finite and vice versa. It is the miracle of all miracles, namely the miracle of essential love (which alone through self-opposition can unite with itself) or the miracle of God's livingness and realness." [8] Nature is God in the actuality of His self-love. Both life and love are terrestrial expressions of God.

This is a truth which gradually becomes clearer. As with every vital development which I have traced, love also has an advancing history. Wordsworth is acutely aware of love's central importance in the growth of a poet's mind. As a child, he experiences "silent, inobtrusive sympathies"; as a mature poet, he reaches the "height of feeling intellect." [9] Love begins more or less unconsciously:

7. Schelling, 7, 60.
8. *6*, 63–4; 7, 59.
9. *The Prelude*, II, 316; XIII, 205.

Even then the common haunts of the green earth,
With the ordinary human interests
Which they embosom, all without regard
As both may seem, are fastening on the heart
Insensibly, each with the other's help,
So that we love, not knowing that we love,
And feel, not knowing whence our feeling comes.[1]

"Thus daily were my sympathies enlarged," and in due course

There came a time of greater dignity
Which had been gradually prepar'd, and now

1. Ibid., VIII, 166–72. Even more striking is Wordsworth's insistence that love enters into our very first perceptions of the world. That is his main point about the infant babe. Here Wordsworth himself presents my argument most clearly, so I will be pardoned for quoting at length:

Thus, day by day,
Subjected to the discipline of love,
His organs and recipient faculties
Are quicken'd, are more vigorous, his mind spreads,
Tenacious of the forms which it receives.
In one beloved presence, nay and more,
In that most apprehensive habitude
And those sensations which have been deriv'd
From this beloved Presence, there exists
A virtue which irradiates and exalts
All objects through all intercourse of sense.

. . . . .

From nature largely he receives; nor so
Is satisfied, but largely gives again,
For feeling has to him imparted strength,
And powerful in all sentiments of grief,
Of exultation, fear, and joy, his mind,
Even as an agent of the one great mind,
Creates, creator and receiver both,
Working but in alliance with the works
Which it beholds.—Such, verily, is the first
Poetic spirit of our human life;
By uniform control of after years
In most abated or suppress'd, in some,
Through every change of growth or of decay,
Pre-eminent till death. [*The Prelude*, II, 250–60, 267–80.]

Rush'd in as if on wings, the time in which
The pulse of Being everywhere was felt,
When all the several frames of things, like stars
Through every magnitude distinguishable,
Were half confounded in each other's blaze,
One galaxy of life and joy. Then rose
Man, inwardly contemplated, and present
In my own being, to a loftier height;
As of all visible natures crown; and first
In capability of feeling what
Was to be felt; in being rapt away
By the divine effect of power and love.

Finally, looking back over the course of his spiritual growth, Wordsworth says in the last book of *The Prelude,*

Imagination having been our theme,
So also hath that intellectual love,
For they are each in each, and cannot stand
Dividually.[2]

In neither Wordsworth nor Schelling did intellectual love last. Enthusiasm has meager chances of longevity within the life of any single individual. ("By uniform control of after years In most abated or suppress'd.") It is primarily a youthful point of view. It is true that every spiritual orientation selects experience which corroborates itself and rejects experience which does not. From this standpoint, every Weltanschauung is self-sustaining. But, as Hegel has tried to show us, life does not stand still. It is primarily a feat of youth to reject all radical finitude and radical evil. Youth can say yes to the world enthusiastically, and it can continue to say yes for a considerable time. The rejection of radical evil demands the youthful qualities of excessive energy and deficient experience. But, of course,

2. *The Prelude,* II, 181; VIII, 623-36; XIII, 185-8.

youth is not a matter of years. The change from youth to maturity *is* a change of Weltanschauung. To say that Wordsworth and Schelling changed because they grew up is not to disparage the earlier viewpoint. Perhaps the earlier viewpoint is the more correct one.

Yet the fact remains that both Wordsworth and Schelling probably changed their points of view because the fact of radical evil forced its way into their experience. I have already discussed this point at some length in relation to the death of Wordsworth's brother, John. It lends our account a somber note to discover that four years later Wordsworth's experience fell to Schelling. In 1809, Schelling's wife, Karoline, died:

> This event signified incontestably a turning point in his life. With the loss of the completely loving and understanding, mother-like wife, who lived constantly in his thoughts, he lost the real center of his existence. At that time he used to express the wish to retire completely from public life. His philosophical productivity seemed to be extinguished. In the remaining forty-three years of his life, Schelling did not publish a single sizable philosophic work.[3]

Enthusiasm leaves out something important. It exists in the happy time when human evil lies quiescent and seems gathered up in the goodness of things.

3. Hermann Zeltner, *Schelling* (Stuttgart, Frommanns, 1954), p. 38. The bulk of Schelling's later philosophy was published posthumously.

7. *Both-And Logic in the Immortality Ode*

I DELIBERATELY REFRAINED, in the foregoing pages, from citing tempting passages of the Immortality Ode, because I wished to examine it freshly and in detail without having committed myself to definite interpretations of individual passages. I wanted to avoid making the poet's attitude more important than his poem. If a typological study is to be genuinely helpful in textual interpretation, it is important to avoid confusing instrumental and final values and to acknowledge that the type is not an end in itself but a heuristic instrument which helps the investigator order details and resolve problems of meaning and emphasis. The danger is that one may come to see only the type in every text, so that the latter becomes merely an illustrative document instead of the primary object of study. But as long as this pitfall is avoided, the type may be an invaluable guide for illuminating a text in all its individual complexity. In textual interpretation, the type is like the Kantian Idea of Reason; it is a guiding principle useful for ordering knowledge but not in itself an object of knowledge.

There is, of course, no assurance that the Enthusiastic type of outlook *is* a trustworthy guide for confronting the

Ode. Everything depends upon the adequacy with which
it actually helps the reader make sense of the text. But, on
the basis of external evidence, we may assume in advance
that the Ode is *probably* expressive of the viewpoint ana-
lyzed in the previous pages. This preliminary probability
derives from the poem's date of composition (1802–04),
which falls well within the period with which this study
has dealt.[1] But external evidence can never be decisive in
determining meaning. I would not, for example, argue
that the poem divides into two distinct sections simply because the poet composed the first four stanzas in 1802 and
the final seven ones about two years later. Indeed, in the
case of the Ode, these external, biographical facts have
tended to blind us to the poem's essential unity and have
hindered rather than helped the interpretation of its meaning. And if the mere fact of interrupted composition has
nothing to tell us with regard to a poem's unity of mood
and meaning, then neither does a mere date of composition assure us that the poet is writing from the same viewpoint which characterizes his other poetry of the period.
De Selincourt's early dating of the poem merely lends
additional support to the "Enthusiastic" or affirmative
interpretation of the Ode which I believe to be the correct
one. That interpretation must, however, justify itself on
the basis of the text alone. My hope is that the "text alone"
will appear more perspicuous and less problematical in
the light of the previous pages.

Before discussing the Ode stanza by stanza, it will be
helpful to describe briefly its general pattern. The general
structure is dramatically determined. That is to say, the
Ode is a re-enactment of thoughts and feelings which occu-
pied the poet in a concrete situation: a solitary sojourn in
a familiar valley between sunrise and sunset on a bright
spring day. The first two stanzas begin the poem in medias

1. This is de Selincourt's dating of the poem, and it remains the most
authoritative conjecture we possess. See Wordsworth, *4*, 464–5.

res. They announce the overt theme (the departed freshness of childhood) in the form of a meditation. Then, in
stanzas 3 and 4, the poet describes the springtime scene
which has prompted his meditation and he reiterates the
question which the scene has caused him to ask: "Whither
is fled the visionary gleam?" In order to answer this question, the poet once again loses himself in thought and only
indirectly refers to the actual scene around him. In this
reverie which comprehends the central five stanzas of the
poem (5–9), the poet answers his question to his own satisfaction, and when he once again (now later in the day)
looks at the scene around him (stanza 10) he finds in it a
deeper meaning than before (stanza 11).

The Ode is thus both meditative and dramatic; it alter-
nates in four deliberate movements between internal musings and external observations, and the final effect of these
alternations is to demonstrate dramatically the interdependence in the poet's Imagination of "active" thought
and "passive" observation. This interdependence is further
demonstrated by the character of the four movements. The
meditative stanzas refer to common sights like those actually surrounding the poet. His musings about childhood are
prompted not only by the springtime landscape but by the
position of the sun. (Note the references to sunrise in the
first half of the poem.) On the other hand, the descriptive
stanzas go far beyond mere *reportage* to the imaginative
significance of the actual scene. For example, in the final
stanza, which strikes a perfect balance between the dramatic and meditative modes, the setting sun of the actual
scene and the period of old age are quite indistinguishable.
The natural scene both occasions and symbolizes the poet's
thoughts.

I call attention to the Ode's dramatic structure because
a grasp of this will solve some of the less essential problems
which the reader frequently encounters. I am thinking par-
ticularly of the "timely utterance" passage in stanza 3.

What was the utterance? It has been suggested that it was a poem written by Wordsworth about the same time he was writing the first four stanzas of the Ode.[2] But such an explanation is circumstantially improbable and ought to be adopted only as a last resort. I do not know of any other passage in Wordsworth which requires for its understanding an autobiographical fact not expressed in the poetry itself. To insist that Wordsworth's meaning here depends upon such esoteric knowledge is false to the spirit in which he composed and, indeed, amounts to a derogation of his literary tact and competence. It is, furthermore, a quite unnecessary hypothesis, since a far simpler explanation suggests itself from the text alone.

The explanation was first suggested to me by part of a note from Professor Pottle: "Isn't the utterance precisely stanzas 1 and 2? The poem starts with no setting, no 'now.' The poet is in a reverie, and the matter of the reverie is grief for a loss." Pottle's suggestion begins to seem convincing as soon as we attend to the poem's dramatic structure. The first two stanzas present the poet's reverie. Then, in the third stanza, the poet snaps out of his reverie to contemplate and describe the scene around him. In general, stanza 3 is concerned with both the natural scene and the effect which the scene is having on the poet, and the lines about the timely utterance follow this general pattern. The poet is speaking of the effect which the landscape has just had and is having upon him. Notice, in support of this, the curious way in which the poet shifts tenses at the beginning of stanza 3. The stanza begins with a "Now":

> Now, while the birds thus sing a joyous song,
> And while the young lambs bound
> As to the tabor's sound,

2. See H. W. Garrod, *Wordsworth* (2d ed. London, Oxford Univ. Press, 1927), p. 113; Lionel Trilling, "The Immortality Ode" in *The Liberal Imagination*, New York, Doubleday, 1950.

But suddenly the poet changes tense: "To me alone there came a thought of grief"; then changes back again: "And I again am strong." The simplest explanation of the shifts is that the poet alludes to an event which has just taken place in the present dramatic setting. The springtime scene, with a shepherd boy who reminds him of his own departed youth, has just put him in a brown study by making him realize how different he has become. He uttered that melancholy feeling: "It is not now as it hath been of yore." The timely externalizing ("utterance") of the thought of grief has had a cathartic effect ("gave that thought relief"), and the poet snaps out of his reverie to notice his surroundings and to comment on what has just taken place: "Now, in this setting, I *had* a melancholy thought; I uttered it (see stanzas 1 and 2) and I again am strong." This interpretation is further supported by a second allusion in stanza 3 to the poet's momentary lapse: *"No more* shall grief of mine the season wrong."

The dramatic pattern of the Ode is, however, far less problematical than its thematic pattern. It is all too easy to read the poem as a melancholy development of the time-worn *ubi-sunt* theme. "Où sont les neiges d'antan?" "Where is it now, the glory and the dream?" But Wordsworth's poem is distinct from the *ubi-sunt* tradition in one important respect. For him the question is not merely rhetorical; he does not simply express a nostalgic regret for that which can never come again. Instead, he seriously tries to answer the question, and, one may add, actually answers it to his own satisfaction.[3] But even the reader who detects

3. The very fact that lost freshness disturbs and puzzles the poet is indicative. Ordinarily the experience is simply a source of regret and nostalgia. One realizes that, as time goes on, continued freshness (almost a *contradictio in adjecto*) becomes impossible. But Enthusiasm refuses to accept the fact that time goes on in the ordinary sense. When it confronts an apparently radical change like death or lost freshness, it has to probe deeper to discover why the change is not, ultimately, radical.

something unique in the earnestness with which Wordsworth asks his question may still miss the special quality
of the answer which the Ode presents. The answer seems
to be this: <u>in childhood we once had a glimpse of a glorious ideal, but in maturity all that sustains us is the memory of that ideal.</u> Life in maturity is not all it might be,
but let us give thanks that through memory we can still
preserve something of the joy and fulfillment we once felt.
This kind of meaning is present in the Ode, and it would
be an oversimplification to disregard such somber feelings
of regret and diminishment. But it would be a still greater
oversimplification to miss the preponderant mood of joy
and affirmation. Even though <u>the obvious theme of the
poem is that of loss, we should not overlook the countertheme which at every point subtly denies loss.</u> Wordsworth
insists (and this should not surprise us) on having it both
ways. <u>His poem about lost glory is unmistakably characterized by brightness not only in its imagery and diction
but also in its essential meaning.</u> The very strategy with
which he laments lost glory assures us that glory will always persist. As Cleanth Brooks first pointed out, the characteristic mode of the poem is that of paradox.[4]

Indeed, the basic meaning of the poem is paradoxical:
what is gone is not gone; the source of regret is really a
source of gratitude. But a paradox is not a contradiction; it
is an apparent contradiction which we ultimately understand to be the deepest truth. <u>The aim of the Immortality
Ode is to demonstrate</u> that what appears to be a contradiction is really a paradox: that glory is both lost and not lost.
The logic of the poem is the imaginative logic of both-and.

That is exactly what the Ode brilliantly does. This trait of Enthusiasm
also suggests why the Ode is about immortality as well as lost glory, for
the Ode is a *general* affirmation that in the deepest sense time and change
are not radical.

4. See Cleanth Brooks, "Wordsworth and the Paradox of the Imagination" in *The Well Wrought Urn,* New York, Harcourt, 1947.

Its aim exemplifies the primary goal of Enthusiasm which is to reconcile contraries. The burden of my analysis will be to show how Wordsworth attempts this sort of reconciliation not only in the final stanzas but, implicitly, throughout the poem.

In order to lend force to the final reconciliation with which the Ode ends, Wordsworth uses a consistent rhetorical strategy: he takes away with one hand what he seems to be giving with the other. Wherever his overt theme is one of loss he advances a covert countertheme which, through imagery or diction, subtly denies loss. Or, in a variation of this technique, he sometimes expresses loss in a way so obviously paradoxical that the reader is made to feel that the loss itself is paradoxical. These techniques are at work (in widely different degrees) at every point in the Ode, and the reader will forgive me if I analyze the poet's pervasive strategy in some detail.

The first stanza seems on the surface to be nothing but a "thought of grief" in the face of life's mutability ("It is not now as it hath been of yore. . . . The things which I have seen I now can see no more"), and there can be no doubt that the primary thought of the stanza is one of grief. But in its very expression the grief is qualified and delimited. For, how is it that the poet knows that the "celestial light" has disappeared? Because, as he tells us, he now looks at those selfsame universal things which he saw as a child and no longer senses in them the freshness they used to have. There is nothing in the first stanza about external mutability, no dismay that the landscape has been marred by mills and tenements. Indeed, it is precisely because nothing has changed in nature that the poet knows something has changed in himself. There is, therefore, a subtle and not entirely accidental contradiction between the first and last parts of the stanza. The poet certainly can see the *things* which he has seen, for these are common sights like meadows, groves, and streams, things which can "never change or die." The only external changes mentioned in the stanza are those of night and day, which like all the other alternations of nature are cyclical and constant. The poet "explains" his sense of change by calling attention to that which is changeless. I do not wish to imply that we should take lightly Wordsworth's expression of loss and regret, but we should also be aware that the affirmative countertheme is present from the very first lines.

The implicit countertheme is even more evident in the second stanza. Here the poet calls particular attention to the fact that he is apparently contradicting himself:

> The sunshine is a *glorious* birth;
> But yet I know, where'er I go,
> That there hath past away a *glory* from the earth.

Even the structure of the stanza is illustrative of this both-and kind of meaning. In the first seven lines the poet enumerates various "common sights" which have remained and will remain "glorious" to him. Then, in the final two lines, he laments the glory which is gone. The reader, of course, understands that the poet must be speaking of two different kinds of glory, and, indeed, on one level he is. But the poet's refusal to make a verbal distinction between the two glories suggests (or lends force to the later suggestion) that the two glories are ultimately the same after all, that in a deeper sense nothing has changed. Again, this affirmative note should not be emphasized at the expense of the poet's negation, which is given the position of emphasis at the end of the stanza; but, on the other hand, the idea of change is being implicitly qualified by the constancy of nature. The rainbow still comes and goes (how dependable and cyclical of it!), the rose still blooms, and the sun rises every morning. These common sights will never change; they are available in every period of a man's life.

If the reader has not already objected to my analysis of Wordsworth's "thought of grief" in stanzas 1 and 2, I should like to forestall a quite justifiable objection. The analysis seems to imply that Wordsworth is carefully setting up a straw man simply in order to knock him down at the end of the poem. Although this kind of reading is far from my own understanding of the poem, it is extremely difficult to avoid the trap of all discursive analysis, which is that everything must be laid open. Discursiveness and explicitness are synonymous. In the early stanzas of the poem the denial of loss remains latent and inexplicit, while the feeling of loss is brought out with force. But analysis can only point to this subtle quality in the poetry; it cannot imitate it. In the body of the Ode itself, there is a genuine tension between that which was and that which is, and through this tension we feel the power of the final reconciliation. Analysis, however, collapses the tension by making the implicit explicit. It reconciles the opposites too soon. Nevertheless, it is essential to point to the subtle workings of Wordsworth's countertheme, since it is only through this implicit agency that the final reconciliation is honestly justified. Too often the critic of the poem, missing the preparations that have gone before, finds the affirmative conclusion unconvincing or even overlooks entirely its predominantly affirmative character. The countertheme must be recognized not only in order to grasp the poem's doctrinal content but also in order to appreciate its artistic unity. Everything in the final stanzas is prepared for in the earlier ones. Thematically, the Ode is like an organic growth: at first the meaning is merely latent, but gradually through a process of development the primary idea of the poem comes into full view.

stanza 3

After the theme of loss has been introduced in the first two stanzas, the poet turns to the joyous landscape. He has chosen the springtime scene as the dramatic setting for his poem not only in order to contrast it with his momentary spiritual winter but also in order to suggest the possibility of a renewal in himself comparable to that which constantly recurs in visible nature. The whole of stanza 3 is a demonstration of the poet's spiritual renewal through his sympathetic participation in that of nature. What the poet sees in nature he feels echoed in himself. That is the reason the poet explicitly places himself in the landscape he is describing. He does not merely report the natural event (the echoes, for example); he tells the way the event corresponds to something in his own soul. Nature announces its joy and vitality through the trumpeting cataracts, and the rest of nature echoes the sounds: "I hear the Echoes through the mountains throng." The poet hears. That is to say, something in his soul responds to or echoes the sounds just as the mountains echo them. The external processes of nature correspond to its internal processes within the poet. The whole of stanza 3 exhibits the Imagination at work, performing its appointed job which is sympathetically to correlate and fuse the external and internal. Notice this effect in the next line: "The Winds come to me from the fields of sleep." The winds come from the dormant winter, one supposes, or, in any case, from a place where *they* have been dormant, and they blow over the earth to awaken everything into life. Both the winds and the sounds announce the awakening and prompt it. Imaginatively, the physical winds correspond to feelings and memories which have lain dormant but which, prompted by the scene, reawaken the poet's spirit. The cataracts, echoes, winds, and the shouts of the shepherd boy have a mnemonic effect which causes the poet to participate in the "jollity" of the universal renewal.

In stanza 4 the poet develops this theme of participation. "I have heard the call" means "I have heard what you shout to each other, and I remember. I hear the message which it has for me." And because he has heard, the poet has been taken out of his spiritual isolation to feel what the "blessed creatures" feel. Nevertheless, his participation is partly an effort of will, and he suggests this by recalling once more his previous thought of grief:

> Oh evil day! if I were sullen
> While Earth herself is adorning,
> This sweet May-morning.

The poet must strain to experience the joy and freshness which is vouchsafed effortlessly to the blessed creatures, and this straining is reflected in the shrill repetitiveness of:

> The fulness of your bliss, I feel—I feel it all.
>
> . . . . .
>
> I hear, I hear, with joy I hear!

We do not have to doubt the genuineness of the poet's participation, but we should notice how carefully he has exhibited the effort of will which the participation requires. Just as Wordsworth has qualified his thought of grief by calling attention to nature's constant glory, he has also qualified his joy in nature by pointing to the difference between the child's instinctive gaiety and his own joy which demands the poet's sympathetic Imagination.

In another, more significant respect the poet's joy (as presented in stanza 4) differs from that of the child. The mature man's sense of participation in the sweet May morning does not derive simply from his experience of the scene before him nor simply from his memory of the joyous feelings which the springtime used to elicit from him. Both of these make his participation possible, but the participation itself is now different from what it was. In former days the poet rejoiced like the shepherd boy in a direct, immediate experience of nature's glory; but now his joy resides not in the particular objects before him but in their universal or "philosophical" significance. For example, the shepherd boy in the actual scene becomes in the poet's Imagination "the children." The particular valley in which he finds himself becomes "a thousand valleys far and wide." The "Babe" and "Mother" stand for all infants and mothers, rather than figures before him. This universalizing tendency in stanza 4 suggests that although the poet can no longer feel the freshness of individual objects, he can, unlike the child, sympathize consciously with the universal life of things. His joy, being more expansive and conscious, is in a sense even more significant than the child's joy. The poet's language hints at an "abundant recompense."

Even the final, negative lines of stanza 4 express a regret which is qualified by the character of the poet's language:

> —But there's a Tree, of many, one,
> A single Field which I have looked upon,
> Both of them speak of something that is gone:
> The Pansy at my feet
> Doth the same tale repeat:
> Whither is fled the visionary gleam?
> Where is it now, the glory and the dream?

Just as in stanza 2, Wordsworth introduces his negative thought with a "But" (this in spite of the fact that he has promised no more to wrong the season with a thought of grief), and again the "But" points to the apparent contradiction between the affirmative and negative parts of the stanza. He has just affirmed that he feels *all* the old childhood feelings (l. 41), and now he contradicts himself by saying that something is gone. As in stanza 2, the apparent contradiction can be explained on one level by saying that the joy which remains is different from that which is gone, but the prima facie contradiction suggests that the two kinds of joy are at once different and the same. Furthermore, it is significant that the poet severely limits that which is gone to the *single* tree, field and pansy, while his previous affirmation of the joy which remains comprehended the whole of nature. A clue to the poet's meaning in these lines is provided by the phrase "which I have looked upon." The single objects he refers to were evidently familiar to him as a child. The poet finds himself in the valley in which he used to play, and the old scene brings home to him the fact that he no longer can look upon that tree and field with "aching joys" and "dizzy raptures." But, notice that the old familiar tree is but one "of many"; only the particular objects of experience have lost their freshness. Wordsworth emphasizes that this is an important loss, but his language, by pointing out the particularity of the loss, also hints that it is neither radical nor unrecompensed. Poised against the child's "single field," the countertheme makes itself felt in the "thousand valleys" of the mature poet.

In the first four stanzas Wordsworth has presented two kinds of glory: one, the child's, is immediate and particularized, while the other, the mature man's, is generalized and mediated by thought and memory. At the end of these four stanzas the poet asks, "whither is fled the visionary gleam," the freshness and delight of childhood? The ostensible purpose of the central five stanzas which follow is to answer this question, but the question has already been answered implicitly: the visionary gleam has fled to the poet's Imagination, to the "philosophic mind." The real task of the central stanzas is not to amplify this answer but rather to show why the two kinds of glory are not radically different. The sense of contrast and opposition between childhood and maturity is gradually to be transformed into a sense of beneficent, teleological continuity. The two moments are to be bridged by showing them as stages in a continuous, cyclical, and self-identical process.

In Stanza 2 the poet touched lightly on the apparent contradiction that glory is both lost and not lost. In Stanza 5, he begins abruptly with an explicit paradox: "Our birth is but a sleep and a forgetting." To gain an idea of the poet's paradoxical intent, we need only recall the brilliant picture he has just presented of springtime vitality. Birth is an *awakening* into life from the fields of sleep. The "Babe *leaps* up on his Mother's arm"; "all the earth is gay." That is what birth and rebirth normally signify to the poet. What Wordsworth means in stanza 5, of course, is that the state of pre-existence when we are united with God is the highest and most glorious form of life we can know. Compared to that stage of existence, everything else is a sleep. On the other hand, life before birth lies in the fields of sleep. The effect of the line is to imply that our birth is a sleep *and* an awakening. And, as if to call further attention to his paradox, the poet again deliberately (if not completely) contradicts himself. Even though birth is a "forgetting" we come "not in entire forgetfulness."

This paradoxical mode in the central stanzas has two main functions. The first is fairly obvious: by employing paradox, the poet re-enforces his paradoxical meaning— lost glory is not lost; death is not death. Paradox is one way of expressing a both-and sort of meaning. The second function is similar but more subtle. The paradoxes of stanzas 5–9 all seem to disparage the later stages of life; pre-existence is praised at the expense of birth, childhood at the expense of maturity, but the paradoxical way in which the later stage is disparaged really constitutes praise in disguise. On a literal level, the poet seems to place *all* value on pre-existence and childhood, but his very purpose in doing so is to glorify the later stage as well. The extravagance with which the poet denigrates earthly, actual existence in order to explain its lost glory is really a device for praising earthly life.

Wordsworth is quite explicit in viewing his doctrine of pre-existence (whether or not he believed in it) as a poetical device: "Archimedes said that he could move the world if he had a point whereon to rest his machine. . . . I took hold of the notion of pre-existence as having sufficient foundation in humanity for authorizing me to make for my purpose the best use of it I could as a Poet." [5] The resting place outside the world for Wordsworth's poetical lever is a state of perfect fusion with God. The doctrine of pre-existence serves to glorify postnatal existence in the same way that, psychologically, Enthusiasm's brief moments of fusion serve to sustain its confident striving. The doctrine does this for one reason alone: the movement from God our home into life is not a radical change for us. In fact, both stages of existence are part of life's perfect continuity. In stanza 5, at the very moment when the poet seems to assert that birth is a change for the worse, his imagery proclaims that it is not, strictly speaking, a change at all. The main image of stanza 5 is the apparent path of the sun around the earth. (One could even say that this is the controlling image of the whole poem, since it recurs in all three sections and symbolizes two of the poem's central ideas: nature's eternal cyclicity and man's unbroken spiritual history.)

> The Soul that rises with us, our life's Star,
>   Hath had elsewhere its setting,
>   And cometh from afar.

Although the image implies a doctrine of palingenesis, its main function here is to signify the self-identity of the

5. From the Fenwick note to the poem, Wordsworth, *4*, 464.

sun (soul) through all the stages of its diurnal course. It is the same sun at morning and evening, and it remains the same in the antipodes (after death and before birth). The different stages of the sun-soul are all part of a continuum and have, therefore, "another and finer connection than that of contrast."

> It is a connection formed through the subtle process by which, both in the natural and the moral world, qualities pass insensibly into their contraries, and things revolve upon each other. As, in sailing upon the orb of this planet, a voyage towards the regions where the sun sets, conducts gradually to the quarter where we have been accustomed to behold it come forth at its rising; and, in like manner, a voyage towards the east, the birth-place in our imagination of the morning, leads finally to the quarter where the sun is last seen when he departs from our eyes; so the contemplative Soul, travelling in the direction of mortality, advances to the country of everlasting life; and, in like manner, may she continue to explore those cheerful tracts, till she is brought back, for her advantage and benefit, to the land of transitory things—of sorrow and of tears.[6]

Even though stanza 5 ostensibly shows that glory fades because we travel further from the source of glory, it also subtly suggests that the process of fading is not unidirectional. Why does the poet stop at high noon? Does not the sun gradually return to the horizon? And, if clouds of glory appear at sunrise, are there not also "Clouds that gather round the setting sun" (l. 197)? Since stanza 5 presumably "shows" why glory fades, it would be premature of the poet to carry the sun further in its path. Yet, he has care-

6. "Upon Epitaphs" in *The Prose Works of William Wordsworth*, ed. A. B. Grosart (3 vols. London, Noxon, 1876), 2, 30–1.

fully introduced the principle for his final affirmation of
continued glory by the imagery with which he explains its
loss. Furthermore, he insists openly that the loss is very
gradual:

> The Youth, who daily farther from the east
>   Must travel, still is Nature's Priest,
>   And by the vision splendid
>   Is on his way attended.

Very slowly, the clouds of recollection which illuminate
the morning sky depart and the prison-house shades of intellect and habit close about the young man, who all but
loses his instinctive connection with the life of things.

The light of common day would seem to be the hours
from about 11:30 to 3:00, the period after the morning
clouds have dispersed and before the evening ones have
gathered. This is the period of young manhood (described
at length in *The Prelude*) when the light of intellect
proudly evaporates the clouds of childhood feelings:

> Thus strangely did I war against myself,
> A Bigot to a new Idolatry
> Did like a Monk who hath forsworn the world
> Zealously labour to cut off my heart
> From all the sources of her former strength.[7]

The young man stands equidistant and, therefore, at the
farthest point from his source and his destination. At that
moment the soul senses its greatest autonomy as well as
its greatest isolation and emptiness. Trying to cast aside
emotion and deeper religious feelings, it relies wholly on
logical analysis and thinks that unaided it can solve life's
problems and set life's goals. This moment is crucial since
it seems to endanger life's continuity, but even though
young manhood is furthest from the truth, it is, neverthe-

7. *The Prelude*, XI, 74–7.

less, a necessary stage in the teleological development toward the philosophic mind. In each stage the soul retains her self-identity. As the imagery of stanza 5 suggests, one sort of light gives way to another, but it is still the light of the sun.

However, one should not underestimate the danger of "common day." Many a man permanently cuts off his heart from all the sources of his former strength, and everyone might do so were it not for memory and visible nature, which work in conjunction to prevent us from losing connection with our earlier selves and the source of things. In *The Prelude,* Wordsworth speaks of high noon as an eclipse:

> What then remained in such eclipse? what light
> To guide or chear? The laws of things which lie
> Beyond the reach of human will or power;
> The life of nature, by the God of love
> Inspired, celestial presence ever pure;
> These left, the Soul of Youth must needs be rich,
> Whatever else be lost, and these were mine,
> Not a deaf echo, merely, of the thought
> Bewilder'd recollections, solitary,
> But living sounds. Yet in despite of this,
> This feeling, which howe'er impair'd or damp'd,
> Yet having been once born can never die.[8]

The poet's answer is precisely the one implied by the early stanzas of the Immortality Ode: nature remains and reminds, "The life of nature, by the God of love Inspired." The constantly self-renewing scenes of nature serve to keep our lives continuous like the path of the sun or like the arch of the rainbow:

8. Ibid., XI, 96–107. The syntax is not altogether clear, but the main force of the passage is not difficult to perceive.

My heart leaps up when I behold
  A rainbow in the sky:
So was it when my life began;
So is it now I am a man;
So be it when I shall grow old,
  Or let me die!
The Child is father of the Man;
And I could wish my days to be
Bound each to each by natural piety.

Wordsworth later chose the last three lines of this lyric as the epigraph to the Ode because the two poems make the same basic point. Like the sun's path, the rainbow's arch represents the very continuity it sustains. Just as nature is always the same so, thanks in part to its constancy, is man's soul as it traverses *its* path from horizon to horizon and beyond.

Because visible nature performs this important role, it must surprise us to encounter the mild derogation of "Earth" in stanza 6.

The homely Nurse doth all she can
To make her Foster-child, her Inmate Man,
  Forget the glories he hath known.

Yet the first four stanzas, which show visible nature doing all she can to make us *remember,* simply contradict this accusation! The contradiction is, however, of a piece with all the other paradoxes which have gone before. On one level Earth's pleasurable distractions ("in her own natural kind") make us forget the imperial or supernatural glories which underlie nature and man. Our real home is with infinitude and only there. But on another level, Earth's natural yearnings are supernatural ones in disguise. The difference between the "imperial palace" and our foster home is one of stage, not essence, for the poet as well as the child is able to look *through* nature to the divine significance of her natural yearnings. The homely nurse may "do all she can" to make us forget, but the poet nowhere goes so far as to say that she succeeds in her aim. The ultimate effect of Earth's beauty is to make us remember the very thing she tries to make us forget. That is why the poet adopts a benignant tone toward the foster mother; her pleasures are really terrestrial counterparts of the pleasures in the imperial palace. Earth's loving influence has an effect which, paradoxically, defeats her natural yearnings, for by innocently following her maternal instincts she nourishes and sustains the child's religious feelings. Of course, whenever life advances to a new stage, something desirable (though inessential) is always partially lost. In this case Earth both causes our loss *and* prevents it from being complete. Praise of the imperial palace—something beyond the world—is really praise of this world ("in which, in the end, We find our happiness or not at all"). All of Earth's maternal attempts to distract us from former glory really direct the mind to present glory.

In stanza 7, the poet is still concerned with those distractions which make us forget the imperial palace; however, it is now the child's human mother who distracts him. Again, such distractions do not really endanger the child's religious feelings; they are, in fact, as *The Prelude* tells us, essential to their proper development. Like Earth, the child's parents exercise a loving influence:

> Frettied by sallies of his mother's kisses,
> With light upon him from his father's eyes!

Far from diminishing the child's glory, this "discipline of love" is essential to its development.

> Thus, day by day,
> Subjected to the discipline of love,

His [the child's] organs and recipient faculties
Are quicken'd, are more vigorous, his mind spreads,
Tenacious of the forms which it receives.
In one beloved presence, nay and more,
In that most apprehensive habitude
And those sensations which have been deriv'd
From this beloved Presence, there exists
A virtue which irradiates and exalts
All objects through all intercourse of sense.[9]

The poet explains how the child is turned away from the visionary gleam by describing the process "Whereby this infant sensibility, Great birthright of our Being, [is in us] Augmented and sustain'd" (ll. 285–7). The terrestrial counterparts of Divine Love actually preserve and re-enforce our birthright rather than diminish it.

As soon as the reader perceives Wordsworth's back-handed strategy, stanza 7 seems less trivial than it must otherwise appear. On the surface, the stanza simply enumerates in a kind of elevated baby talk, the various activities and influences which lure the child from glory. But the whole purpose of the enumeration is to suggest that glory remains with us throughout our lives because the child is father of the man. The attentive reader discovers that the poet quickly ceases to talk of the "six years' Darling of a pigmy size." What should a six-year-old be doing at weddings or funerals or fitting his tongue to dialogues of business or love or strife? The poet is talking about man's whole course of life in such a way that man seems to remain a six-year-old:

The little Actor cons another part;
Filling from time to time his "humorous stage"
With all the Persons, down to palsied Age,
That Life brings with her in her equipage.

9. *The Prelude*, II, 250–60.

The child evidently forgets his true nature in playing his parts, but the metaphor also affirms that man's soul remains essentially the same throughout his life. The metaphor parallels that of the sun's path, except that here the ages of man are not stages in the sun's circuit but parts played by a child actor. Since the child is father of the man, the latter retains his primal nature, and any glory which accrues to the child must accrue to the man as well.

In the first part of stanza 8, the poet's extravagant praise of the child seems to verge on the absurd. His intention is evidently to disparage maturity with its sobriety and intellectual pretension by pointing to the child's possession of those truths "Which we are toiling all our lives to find." [1] But we may also note that this hyperglorification of the child is not without implicit qualification. The "little child" is, no doubt, a mighty prophet and seer blest to the extent that his joy and freedom reflect an instinctive feeling of life's ultimate truth, but the mature poet is aware of this fact, while the "best philosopher" is not aware of it at all. The "Eye among the blind" paradoxically knows not what he sees; he is only a philosopher *in potentia.* By selecting the child's *wisdom* as the object of exaggerated praise, Wordsworth emphasizes how implicit that wisdom is and how important, therefore, man's whole teleological development is. Because the child's vaunted virtues remain inexplicit and unconscious until he becomes a man, the poet's praise of the child both disparages the man and secretly praises him.

However, the reader cannot gloss over Wordsworth's quite serious disparagement of later life in the final lines of stanza 8:

> Full soon thy Soul shall have her earthly freight,
> And custom lie upon thee with a weight,
> Heavy as frost, and deep almost as life!

1. This is another incidental illustration of Enthusiasm's striving to attain explicitly that which it already implicitly possesses.

This is the darkest point in the Ode and the only un-
qualified assertion of life's diminishment. The lines set
up tensions which, unlike those of previous stanzas, are
not resolved implicitly within the stanza itself. While the
child enjoys heaven-born freedom, the adult, in unmiti-
gated contrast, suffers the "inevitable yoke," which consists not only in the tendency "Of habit to enslave the
mind" but in all sorrow and "all that is at enmity with
joy." Here is the moment in the Ode when the poet
directly confronts the deeper questions which loss of
"glory" merely symbolizes. If life is essentially good and
joyful, why is man weighted down by his experience of
evil and sorrow? Why must he learn that life is *not* a continuity like the arch of the rainbow, that the child's joyous
vision of life is *not* adequate? The poet's answers to these
implicit questions are reserved for the next stanza. His de-
lay in providing them deepens the tone of the poem and
dramatizes the genuineness of the final resolution. But
those answers can carry force only because the countertheme has done its secret work. Only after his previous
paradoxes can the poet meaningfully exclaim at one moment, "Heavy as frost and deep almost as life!" and then
at the next moment, "O Joy!"

The poet's joy is an affirmation of life's continuity despite his loss of childhood delight and liberty. That time
is past, and no adult can honestly retain the radiance
which was once so bright. But the poet does retain the
religious instincts of which the child's delight was merely
a reflection. The real glory of childhood is not delight and
liberty and new-fledged hope, all of which are in themselves worthy to be blest,[2] but rather

obstinate questionings

2. The "most" in "most worthy to be blest" I take to be an intensifying
adverb like "very" rather than a true superlative: "He is most worthy
and deserves praise."

> Of sense and outward things,
> Fallings from us, vanishings,

feelings which connect us to a world beyond the world of sense. The mind has in it something innate, something not given in sense experience, an independent power which guarantees that the soul's origin is divine. These religious overtones have gradually become more apparent. The poet calls the Ode a "song of thanks and praise," that is, a psalm or hymn, and words like "benediction," "blest," and "creed" re-enforce this implication.

The child's "shadowy recollections" of a divinity which lies beyond the world of sense and shines through it are called "High instincts." They are high because they relate to the divine, but they are instincts because, like the philosophic "truths" of stanza 8, they have not yet reached a conscious level. These instincts are a "fountain light." Here the poet openly gives to light the meaning which remained implicit in the sun metaphor. True light is not glory but something which underlies both glory and the light of common day. Light is our sense of divinity. Each stage of life realizes this religious insight in a different way and testifies to our being with God in all the journey of our life. The glory which the child first senses is fundamentally the same as the truth which the "philosophic mind" perceives. Our early instincts later become the poet's awareness of the divine totality to which we belong:

> Hence in a season of calm weather
> Though inland far we be,
> Our Souls have sight of that immortal sea
> Which brought us hither,
> Can in a moment travel thither,
> And see the Children sport upon the shore,
> And hear the mighty waters rolling evermore.

Being closest to the source, the divine sea, the children sport upon the shore, but in their joyful, direct participation they cannot "see," as can the poet, life's divine totality.

The season of calm weather is important to the poet because ordinarily in our harassed lives we lose sight of the vision which the Ode celebrates. Only in a period of peace and solitude, such as that which the poet enjoys in the present pastoral setting, can we have sight of life's continuity, divinity, and harmony. In such a fleeting vision these earthly years seem but moments in eternity. Yet these moments uphold and succor ("cherish") us through all the striving and tumult of daily life. In other words, the seasons of calm weather are themselves types and symbols of the "eternal Silence" which we envision and remember in such seasons.[3] Just as our divine origin ("the eternal Silence") sustains us from birth to death, so do our occasional religious visions (or recollections) uphold us as we carry on life's business, love, and strife. The fleeting vision is Enthusiasm's moment of fusion with the divine. That temporary fusion assures us that we are keeping our heritage and striving for an ordained goal whose attainment is guaranteed. We re-experience those "truths that wake To perish never." Wordsworth brilliantly presents both the metaphysical and the psychological foundation of his confidence and gratitude. Metaphysically the divinity and continuity of life are assured because our noisy years *are* moments in the eternal silence out of which we arose. Psychologically, that continuity is assured by the ever-recurrent fusions with divinity that we experience from birth till death. As always, the essential perfection of this life is assured by reference to a beyond, to a prenatal state of perfect fusion with God or to the eternal Silence. How-

3. The word "season" suggests the dependable, cyclic recurrence of these sustaining, mystical moments.

ever, it should be added that the real focus of Wordsworth's poem is not on the beyond itself *but on the active processes of life which the beyond illuminates.* That
is the reason, I think, that Wordsworth culminates his
vision and the central stanzas of the Ode with an image
which symbolizes *both* life's static perfection *and* its active
processes—the image of the sea.

In *The Prelude* the sea is expressive of the poet's growing "sentiment of Being." In all things he felt one life, "in
the *wave* itself, And mighty *depth* of waters." [4] The sea
suggests both noisy years (we hear the waters) and eternal
silence as a single, dynamic whole. Even the "land" on
which we as adults now stand is part of the "immortal sea"
which the actual sea symbolizes. It is life's source (the children have, presumably, been cast up on the shore) and its
involucrum (like the eternal silence). Life's active diversity
is represented by the waves ("Thou art to me but as a
wave Of the wild sea"), which are a ceaseless, active striving on the surface of a divine reality eternally fulfilled and
eternally the same; below the waves there is the silence
of the "mighty depth of waters." Waves and depths make
up a majestic indivisible whole whose immortal activity
and calm is suggested by the "mighty waters *rolling* evermore."

With this culminating image the poet's vision recedes
and he notices again the springtime setting which occasioned his reverie. However, he no longer looks upon the
scene as he did in the early stanzas. His reverie has taught
him something. He no longer cries "I feel—I feel it all"
because he knows that "nothing can bring back the hour
Of splendour in the grass, of glory in the flower." But he
also knows that his poetic reverie is itself a transmutation
of "glory" to a conscious level:

4. See *The Prelude,* II, 420–34.

We *in thought* will join your throng,
  Ye that pipe and ye that play,
  Ye that through your hearts to-day
  Feel the gladness of the May! [Italics mine.]

The poet has come to learn that his present thoughts are themselves childhood glory in a different form. Instead of grieving for what is lost he finds strength "In the primal sympathy Which having been, must ever be." Childhood joy and feeling have become "strength" and "thought." However, the poet's strength is joyful and affirmative, and his thought, being based on the primal sympathy, is emotive. He has attained "feeling intellect," not cold apperception.[5] The change has not been radical; the child remains father of the man.

It has gradually become clear that the controlling theme of the Ode is identical with that of *The Prelude*: the growth of the human heart. Essentially, the poet has remained the same throughout his life, for everything fundamental in his present attitudes was implicit in his childhood feelings. Nevertheless, his growth has not been a purely internal development but one based on experience, and specifically the experience of pain and death. The poet's strength derives not only from the "primal sympathy" we are born with but also from the "soothing thoughts that spring Out of human suffering." The thoughts are soothing because human suffering evokes a peculiarly human sympathy; we come to feel a bond of love not only with nature but also with our own kind, and this represents a genuine and desirable expansion of the "primal sympathy." What should a child know of death? Although the child's sense of splendor in objects and his "indisposition to bend to the law of death" as applying to himself

5. See *The Prelude*, XIII, 205.

reflect the deepest truth, he fails to grasp the whole of life, which has a moral dimension as well as a metaphysical one. The child knows only the natural world, but the man has come to know the human world as well. His development has been teleological: love of nature leads to love of man. The "philosophic mind" has also a "human heart" which exhibits "tenderness" as well as "joys and fears." Thus, the pansy of stanza 4 has become a source of profounder reflections. Before, it symbolized loss of freshness; now it symbolizes the entire cyclical life of things with all its inevitable changes, its grandeur, power, sadness, joy, and divinity. The poet's thoughts are too deep either for tears or for pure delight, for with the faith that looks through death, he also looks through all individual stages of life in nature and man. His deep-lying thoughts are essentially religious.

Indeed, the Ode has been a religious poem from the very beginning—a song of thanks and praise to God. The "primal sympathy" which remains with us is nothing other than a loving connection with God. This is expressed in childhood by our sense of glory and delight, and in maturity by the "philosophic mind." "High instincts," "shadowy recollections," "the human heart" are all, ultimately, forms of religious love which permit us at every stage to glimpse the profound truth of life. The truth which the "best Philosopher" sees but cannot speak is the same which the poet consciously makes into an Ode. Truth and love are "each in each and cannot stand Dividually." [6] The real glory of life has been love all along. The freshness the child perceived in natural objects was an expression of his love, and in compensation for the poet's loss of freshness he has achieved a deeper and more permanent form of love:

6. See *The Prelude*, XIII, 185–8.

And O, ye Fountains, Meadows, Hills, and Groves,
Forebode not any severing of our loves!
Yet in my heart of hearts I feel your might;
I only have relinquished one delight
To live beneath your more habitual sway.
I love the Brooks which down their channels fret,
Even more than when I tripped lightly as they.

By the way in which he has resolved his question, the poet
has also traced the growth of his mind. The final stanza
deliberately returns to those same common sights which
marked the first lines. Like the poet's own life, the Ode
has simply made more explicit, conscious, and philosophical that which was implicit from the beginning.

I should like now to conclude this final chapter with a
brief résumé of the Ode's doctrinal content as it relates
to the root ideas of Enthusiasm.

God and the World. The ultimate reason that we never
lose our high instincts is that we are always with God and
he with us. We come from God, our home, but earth is
also our home, for God is also here in the world, "a Presence which is not to be put by." All of the poet's references to a God *beyond* the world are qualified by his
Weltfrömmigkeit or natural piety. Heaven is on earth; it
lies about us in our infancy. The morning clouds which
symbolized God's presence do fade into the light of common day, but even then He is still a loving Presence, for
without His immanence the continuity of life would
vanish and no evening clouds would gather round the setting sun. Primal sympathy or religious love is ultimately
a sense that God is within us and works through us, yet,
as Wordsworth's imagery implies, God is both in the world
and beyond it.

Life and Time. What Wordsworth means by "immortality" is to be understood, as one might expect, with reference to these two categories. Even though Wordsworth did not publish his long title until 1815, one cannot doubt that the concept of immortality was important from the very beginning. The word "immortality" (l. 119) was present in the 1807 edition, as were the words "immortal" (l. 164), "eternal" (ll. 113, 114, 156), "perpetual" (l. 135), "evermore" (l. 168); so were the phrases, "which having been must ever be" (l. 183) and "the faith that looks through death" (l. 186). The concept is inevitable, since it connects directly with the special view of life which the Ode affirms. Life is for Wordsworth a universal quality; everything including a rock or stone is part of God's life and therefore has a life of its own. "Life," then, does not connote any quality of consciousness or even of sensibility, but cuts across and bridges the spiritual and physical worlds. It characterizes both, but lacks the special attributes of either. And because life is neither physical nor spiritual in the ordinary sense, the poet can conceive of life before birth and after death. We are from God, part of Him, and our essential divinity can never perish.

Wordsworth's long title is appropriate for still another reason. Since the Ode affirms that our days are bound each to each, its theme is not only continuity but immortality as well. For *earthly* life is a continuity only because life as a whole is. Birth is a change in stage but not in essence, and if birth is not a radical change, then neither is death. Immortality and life's cyclic continuity are corollaries. What has been, is, and shall be. The sun, which is the symbol of time, is also the symbol of eternity, and this holds true for all of visible nature, where we find "those types of renovation and decay which the fields and woods offer to the notice of the contemplative mind." [7] Time moves, but constantly recurs. The Ode, too, is like the

7. "Upon Epitaphs," p. 32.

circuit of the sun; it runs its path and ends where it
began, stanzas 10 and 11 being deliberate reflections of
stanzas 3 and 1. Immortality is continuous cyclicity.

It seems likely that Wordsworth's view of "revolving
immortality" [8] implies a literal palingenesis:

> The Soul that rises with us, our life's Star,
>   Hath had elsewhere its setting.

The more orthodox Coleridge was shocked by Wordsworth's expansion of this idea in the 1807 version of the
poem:

> Thou, over whom thy Immortality
> Broods like the Day, a Master o'er a Slave,
> A Presence which is not to be put by;
>   To whom the grave
> Is but a lonely bed without the sense or sight
>   Of day or the warm light,
> A place of thought where we in waiting lie.

And, in an earlier (MS) version, the "place of thought"
was, significantly, "A living place where we in waiting lie."
But Wordsworth could well afford to submit to Coleridge's
objections by omitting the offending lines. The real emphasis of the Ode is not on the moments of waiting but on
earthly life. Immortality is confirmed by the nature of this
life, not by a report from beyond the grave. Wordsworth's
pirmary interest is life in its actuality, the period from
birth to death. In terms of the poem's real emphases, the
sun's path in the antipodes contracts to a point, a static
beyond.

Imagination. We are born with divine faculties by which
we keep our connection with God: shadowy recollections,
high instincts, primal sympathy. Because we retain these
faculties, every stage of life is worthy to be blest, yet every

8. See *The Ruined Cottage*, ll. 146–54.

stage is not only a moment of fulfillment but also a moment of striving toward a more complete and comprehensive awareness of life's essential perfection:

> the soul,
> Remembering how she felt, but what she felt
> Remembering not, retains an obscure sense
> Of possible sublimity, to which,
> With growing faculties she doth aspire,
> With faculties still growing, feeling still
> That whatsoever point they gain, they still
> Have something to pursue.[9]

An important feature of Imagination in all its forms is not simply that it connects us with divinity, but that it grows. We move to a greater awareness of that which we have known all along. This motif is crucial in the Ode. The movement from childhood feelings to the philosophic mind is teleological. The nonradical changes which cause us to lose glory are really transmutations of that same glory, but, more than this, they bring abundant recompense because increased development is itself a positive good. Our memories of the imperial palace not only preserve the past but also augur for the future.

The faculty of memory which Wordsworth emphasizes in the Ode is *sympathetic* identification with a former state, not simply conscious recollection. Indeed, our "recollections" as children are not conscious at all. Sympathetic identification ("The fulness of your bliss, I feel—I feel it all.") is nothing other than love. It is the sense of fusion in separation which tends to characterize all of Enthusiasm's experience. Memory, Instinct, Imagination are all forms of a pervasive sympathetic force which binds the poet to nature and his days each to each. This primal sympathy is the essential quality of the soul. It connects

9. *The Prelude*, II, 334–41.

us not only to God but to our past and future and to the whole vast life of things which accompanies us on our journey. The Ode is a conscious expression of that "intellectual love" which crowns man's spiritual development as well as a pious affirmation of life's goodness and beauty.

ODE

INTIMATIONS OF IMMORTALITY FROM
RECOLLECTIONS OF EARLY CHILDHOOD

The Child is father of the Man;
And I could wish my days to be
Bound each to each by natural piety.

I

There was a time when meadow, grove, and stream,
The earth, and every common sight,
   To me did seem
  Apparelled in celestial light,
The glory and the freshness of a dream.
It is not now as it hath been of yore;—
  Turn wheresoe'er I may,
   By night or day,
The things which I have seen I now can see no more.

II

  The Rainbow comes and goes,
  And lovely is the Rose,
  The Moon doth with delight
Look round her when the heavens are bare;
  Waters on a starry night

Are beautiful and fair;
The sunshine is a glorious birth;
But yet I know, where'er I go,
That there hath past away a glory from the earth.

III

Now, while the birds thus sing a joyous song,
And while the young lambs bound
As to the tabor's sound,
To me alone there came a thought of grief:
A timely utterance gave that thought relief,
And I again am strong:
The cataracts blow their trumpets from the steep;
No more shall grief of mine the season wrong;
I hear the Echoes through the mountains throng,
The Winds come to me from the fields of sleep,
And all the earth is gay;
Land and sea
Give themselves up to jollity,
And with the heart of May
Doth every Beast keep holiday;—
Thou Child of Joy,
Shout round me, let me hear thy shouts, thou
happy Shepherd-boy!

IV

Ye blessèd Creatures, I have heard the call
Ye to each other make; I see
The heavens laugh with you in your jubilee;
My heart is at your festival,
My head hath its coronal,
The fulness of your bliss, I feel—I feel it all.
Oh evil day! if I were sullen
While Earth herself is adorning,
This sweet May-morning,

And the Children are culling
    On every side,
In a thousand valleys far and wide,
    Fresh flowers; while the sun shines warm,
And the Babe leaps up on his Mother's arm:—
    I hear, I hear, with joy I hear!
    —But there's a Tree, of many, one,
A single Field which I have looked upon,
Both of them speak of something that is gone:
    The Pansy at my feet
    Doth the same tale repeat:
Whither is fled the visionary gleam?
Where is it now, the glory and the dream?

V

Our birth is but a sleep and a forgetting:
The Soul that rises with us, our life's Star,
    Hath had elsewhere its setting,
        And cometh from afar:
    Not in entire forgetfulness,
    And not in utter nakedness,
But trailing clouds of glory do we come
    From God, who is our home:
Heaven lies about us in our infancy!
Shades of the prison-house begin to close
    Upon the growing Boy,
            But He
Beholds the light, and whence it flows,
    He sees it in his joy;
The Youth, who daily farther from the east
    Must travel, still is Nature's Priest,
    And by the vision splendid
    Is on his way attended;
At length the Man perceives it die away,
And fade into the light of common day.

VI

Earth fills her lap with pleasures of her own;
Yearnings she hath in her own natural kind,
And, even with something of a Mother's mind,
    And no unworthy aim,
    The homely Nurse doth all she can
To make her Foster-child, her Inmate Man,
    Forget the glories he hath known,
And that imperial palace whence he came.

VII

Behold the Child among his new-born blisses,
A six years' Darling of a pigmy size!
See, where 'mid work of his own hand he lies,
Frettied by sallies of his mother's kisses,
With light upon him from his father's eyes!
See, at his feet, some little plan or chart,
Some fragment from his dream of human life,
Shaped by himself with newly-learned art;
    A wedding or a festival,
    A mourning or a funeral;
      And this hath now his heart,
    And unto this he frames his song:
      Then will he fit his tongue
To dialogues of business, love, or strife;
    But it will not be long
    Ere this be thrown aside,
    And with new joy and pride
The little Actor cons another part;
Filling from time to time his "humorous stage"
With all the Persons, down to palsied Age,
That Life brings with her in her equipage;
    As if his whole vocation
    Were endless imitation.

VIII

Thou, whose exterior semblance doth belie
  Thy Soul's immensity;
Thou best Philosopher, who yet dost keep
Thy heritage, thou Eye among the blind,
That, deaf and silent, read'st the eternal deep,
Haunted for ever by the eternal mind,—
  Mighty Prophet! Seer blest!
  On whom those truths do rest,
Which we are toiling all our lives to find,
In darkness lost, the darkness of the grave;
Thou, over whom thy Immortality
Broods like the Day, a Master o'er a Slave,
A Presence which is not to be put by;
Thou little Child, yet glorious in the might
Of heaven-born freedom on thy being's height,
Why with such earnest pains dost thou provoke
The years to bring the inevitable yoke,
Thus blindly with thy blessedness at strife?
Full soon thy Soul shall have her earthly freight,
And custom lie upon thee with a weight,
Heavy as frost, and deep almost as life!

IX

  O joy! that in our embers
  Is something that doth live,
  That nature yet remembers
  What was so fugitive!
The thought of our past years in me doth breed
Perpetual benediction: not indeed
For that which is most worthy to be blest;
Delight and liberty, the simple creed
Of Childhood, whether busy or at rest,
With new-fledged hope still fluttering in his breast:—

Not for these I raise
The song of thanks and praise;
But for those obstinate questionings
Of sense and outward things,
Fallings from us, vanishings;
Blank misgivings of a Creature
Moving about in worlds not realised,
High instincts before which our mortal Nature
Did tremble like a guilty Thing surprised:
But for those first affections,
Those shadowy recollections,
Which, be they what they may,
Are yet the fountain light of all our day,
Are yet a master light of all our seeing;
Uphold us, cherish, and have power to make
Our noisy years seem moments in the being
Of the eternal Silence: truths that wake,
To perish never;
Which neither listlessness, nor mad endeavour,
Nor Man nor Boy,
Nor all that is at enmity with joy,
Can utterly abolish or destroy!
Hence in a season of calm weather
Though inland far we be,
Our Souls have sight of that immortal sea
Which brought us hither,
Can in a moment travel thither,
And see the Children sport upon the shore,
And hear the mighty waters rolling evermore.

X

Then sing, ye Birds, sing, sing a joyous song!
And let the young Lambs bound
As to the tabor's sound!
We in thought will join your throng,

Ye that pipe and ye that play,
Ye that through your hearts to-day
Feel the gladness of the May!
What though the radiance which was once so bright
Be now for ever taken from my sight,
Though nothing can bring back the hour
Of splendour in the grass, of glory in the flower;
We will grieve not, rather find
Strength in what remains behind;
In the primal sympathy
Which having been must ever be;
In the soothing thoughts that spring
Out of human suffering;
In the faith that looks through death,
In years that bring the philosophic mind.

XI

And O, ye Fountains, Meadows, Hills, and Groves,
Forebode not any severing of our loves!
Yet in my heart of hearts I feel your might;
I only have relinquished one delight
To live beneath your more habitual sway.
I love the Brooks which down their channels fret,
Even more than when I tripped lightly as they;
The innocent brightness of a new-born Day
Is lovely yet;
The Clouds that gather round the setting sun
Do take a sober colouring from an eye
That hath kept watch o'er man's mortality;
Another race hath been, and other palms are won.
Thanks to the human heart by which we live,
Thanks to its tenderness, its joys, and fears,
To me the meanest flower that blows can give
Thoughts that do often lie too deep for tears.

APPENDIX B

Original Texts of Passages Translated from the German

CHAPTER 1

7, n. 9. Die Philosophie sollte doch endlich die falsche Abneigung gegen die Theologie, die Frucht langer falscher Verbindung los werden, um die wahre Verbindung herzustellen, die in der geschichtlichen Analyse über den ganzen Zusammenhang besteht. Dieser aber liegt darin, dass sie beide aus der menschlichen Lebendigkeit eine Lebens- und Weltanschauung hervorbringen. Wie dasselbe von der Kunst, insbesondere der Dichtung gilt. Sie müssen also alle drei sich korrespondieren. [Dilthey, *8*, 14]

7, n. 1. Die Philosophie selbst ist ihm nur der differenzierteste, selbstbewussteste Ausdruck für viel weiter verbreitete, weniger differenzierte, unbewusste aber faktische Anschauungen. [Jaspers, p. 10]

CHAPTER 2

17, n. 2. Die äussere Welt liegt vor uns aufgeschlagen, um in ihr die Geschichte unseres Geistes wieder zu finden. [*1*, 383]

Es gehört dazu der Zug innerer Liebe und Verwandtschaft deines eignen Geistes mit dem Lebendigen der Natur. [7, 62]

18, n. 7. Auf diesem zugleich subjektiv- und objektiv-, unendlich- und endlich-Seyn beruht das Ich. [4, 289]

19, n. 2. Nicht also Kants Schüler!—Ihnen ist die Welt und die ganze Wirklichkeit etwas, das unserm Geiste ursprünglich fremd, mit ihm keine Verwandtschaft hat, als die zufällige, dass sie auf ihn wirkt. [1, 360]

Der Idealist in diesem Sinn ist einsam und verlassen mitten in der Welt, von Gespenstern überall umgeben. [1, 362]

20, n. 5. Denn da das Bewusstseyn etwas absolut Inneres ist, zwischen welchem und äussern Dingen keine unmittelbare Berührung gedacht werden kann, so sehen wir uns genöthigt zu behaupten, dass wir die Dinge ursprünglich gar nicht ausser uns . . . sondern . . . in uns selbst anschauen. Ist diess, so scheint zwischen innerer und äusserer Welt keine Trennung möglich. Der äussere Sinn also wird sich völlig in den innern auflösen. Und weil Inneres nur im Gegensatz gegen Aeusseres unterschieden wird, so wird mit der äussern Welt auch die innere unvermeidlich zu Grunde gehen. [1, 390-1]

21, n. 6. Hier, im Momente des absoluten Seyns, vereinigt sich die höchste Passivität mit der unbschränktesten Aktivität. [1, 324-5]

Wer daher den Ausdruck fände für eine Thätigkeit, die so ruhig wie die tiefste Ruhe, für eine Ruhe, die so thätig wie die höchste Thätigkeit, würde sich einigermassen in Begriffen der Natur des Vollkommensten annähern. [4, 305]

22, n. 8. Sie sucht sich selbst, aber eben dadurch flieht sie sich selbst. [3, 489]

24, n. 2. Der unmittelbare Zweck der Natur bei dem jetzt beschriebenen Processe ist nur der Process selbst. [2, 514]

Existenz ist Selbstbejahung, und Selbstbejahung ist Existenz. Eins ist ganz gleichbedeutend mit dem andern. [7, 53]

24, n. 4. Hast du daher die Fülle der Existenz gesehen, wie sie für sich selbst ohne Mass und Ziel ist, so erkenne nun auch das innere und göttliche Band der Dinge, und wie sie durch die Einheit des Wesens, zu dem sie gehören, unter sich eins werden. [7, 201]

CHAPTER 3

27, n. 4. Ich reiche Ihnen die Hand zum ewigen Bündnis für das, was unsere gemeinschaftliche Religion ist—Darstellung des Göttlichen in Wissenschaft, Leben und Kunst und Verbreitung der All-anschauung und Befestigung derselben in den Gemüthern der Menschen. [Plitt, 2, 73]

Ist also Philosophie Wissenschaft des Göttlichen. [7, 30]

Dann wird alles einig und eins werden, auch in der Wissenschaft und Erkenntnis: wie schon von Ewigkeit alles einig und eins war im Seyn, und im Leben der Natur. [7, 126]

28, n. 6. Es ist nur eine Welt . . . Ein Universum, in Ansehung desselben aber alles herrlich, wahrhaft göttlich und schön. [4, 314]

Diess ist die Heiligkeit aller Dinge. Das Kleinste ist heilig wie das Grösste. [7, 189]

29, n. 1. Gott ist die gleich ewige Nacht (wenn er in sich allein ist) und der gleich ewige Tag der Dinge. [7, 162; see Fuhrmans, p. 59]

29, n. 2. . . . und wann wird endlich eingesehen werden, dass gegen diese Wissenschaft, welche wir lehren und deutlich erkennen, Immanenz und Transcendenz völlig und gleich leere Worte sind. [2, 377]

30, n. 7. Diese intellektuale Anschauung tritt dann ein, wo wir für uns selbst aufhören Objekt zu seyn, wo, in sich selbst zurückgezogen, das anschauende Selbst mit dem angeschauten identisch ist. [*1*, 319]

32, n. 1. Unterschied zwischen der Natur, sofern sie erscheint (diese ist blosse *Natura naturata*—Natur in ihrer Besonderung und Trennung vom All—als blosser Widerschein vom absoluten All), und der Natur an sich, wiefern sie in das absolute All aufgelöst und Gott in seinem unendlichen Affirmirtseyn ist. [5, 378]

33, n. 2. Vom Unendlichen zum Endlichen—kein Uebergang! Diess war ein Satz der ältesten Philosophie. . . . Erst in spätern Zeitaltern versuchten geistlose Systeme, Mittelglieder zwischen Unendlichkeit und Endlichkeit zu finden. [*1*, 367–8]

33, n. 3. Dieses Philosophieren war fast von Anfang an ein Ringen um das Verhältnis des absoluten und des endlichen Seins, Gottes und der Welt. [Fuhrmans, p. 6]

33, n. 5. Möglich ist offenbar auch eine *theistische* Sicht, die Gott als eigenes Sein, ja als Person, als transzendentes Sein über der Welt nicht leugnet, sondern ganz festhält, um gerade von da aus der Welt einen eindeutigen Akzent zu geben. [Fuhrmans, p. 20]

34, n. 1. Gott als die unendliche Affirmation von sich selbst. [5, 374]

Das unendliche Affirmirtseyn Gottes im All, oder die Einbildung seiner unendlichen Idealität in die Realität als solche, ist die ewige Natur. [5, 377]

Der Akt der Subjekt-Objektivirung geht durch alle Dinge hindurch, und pflanzt sich in den besonderen Formen fort, die, da sie alle nur verschiedene Erscheinungsweisen der allgemeinen und unbedingten, in dieser selbst unbedingt sind. [5, 325]

Nichts . . . ist daher an sich unvollkommen, sondern alles, was ist, gehört, in wiefern es ist, zum Seyn der unendlichen Substanz. . . . Diess ist die Heiligkeit aller Dinge. Das Kleinste ist heilig wie das Grösste. [7, 189]

35, n. 2. Es will mir aber scheinen, als hätte er damit keine strikte Identität von Gott und Welt gemeint, sondern nur das *unaufhebbare Miteinander* von Subjekt und Objekt, von eigenem Sein und Sein der Welt. [Fuhrmans, p. 42]

36, n. 8. Hier—und nur hier—ist er offenbar und gegenwärtig und entschleiert er sich dem, der den Dingen offen ist. [Fuhrmans, p. 44]

36, n. 9. . . . die Natur selbst nur das volle göttliche Daseyn ist, oder Gott in der Wirklichkeit seines Lebens und in seiner Selbstoffenbarung betrachtet. [7, 59]

CHAPTER 4

38, n. 1. Wer nun die Gegenwart Gottes in dem Leben aller Dinge auf geziemende Art ansiehet und Gott über Alles, durch Alles, und in Allem zu verstehen trachtet, wer bei sich selbst anfanget, sich zu erkennen und andere belebte Dinge gegen seine Natur hält, der erblickt endlich in den Tieren, Kräutern und Steinen ein einförmiges Leben. [Oetinger, 2, 31]

39, n. 3. Das positive Prinzip des Lebens . . . ist durch die ganze Schöpfung verbreitet, und durchdringt jedes einzelne Wesen als der gemeinschaftliche Athem der Natur. [2, 503]

39, n. 6. Das Wesentliche aller Dinge . . . ist das Leben; das Accidentelle ist nur die Art ihres Lebens, und auch das Todte in der Natur ist nicht an sich todt—ist nur das erloschene Leben. [2, 500]

40, n. 8. Absolute Ruhe in der Welt—ist ein Unding, alle Ruhe in der Welt ist nur scheinbar. [2, 383]

42, n. 8. Leben ist die Autonomie in der Erscheinung. [*1*, 249]

Es folgt nämlich, dass kein Theil der Natur blosses Seyn, oder ein bloss Bejahtes seyn kann, sondern jeder vielmehr in sich selbst ebenso Selbstbejahung ist wie das Bewusstseyn oder Ich; es folgt, dass jedes Ding, in seinem wahren Wesen gefasst, mit völlig gleicher Gültigkeit als eine Weise des Seyns und als eine Weise des Selbsterkennens und Selbstoffenbarens betrachtet werden kann. Ein Ding existirt, heisst: es behauptet, es bekräftiget sich selbst. [7, 53]

43, n. 3. Wir können also nicht besser thun, als zu behaupten, dass keiner jener entgegengesetzten Processe den andern, sondern dass sie sich beide wechselseitig bestimmen, beide sich wechselseitig das Gleichgewicht halten. [2, 549]

44, n. 7. Es muss also in jeder Organisation die höchste Einheit des Lebensprocesses in Ansehung des Ganzen und zugleich die höchste Individualität des Lebensprocesses in Ansehung jedes einzelnen Organs herrschen. Beides aber lässt sich nicht vereinigen, als wenn man annimmt, dass ein und derselbe Lebensprocess in jedem einzelnen Wesen sich ins Unendliche individualisire. [2, 520]

Dieses Eine in Allem ist erkennbar in jedem Theil der Materie, alles lebt nur in ihm. Aber ebenso unmittelbar gegenwärtig und in jedem Theil erkennbar ist das All in Einem, wie es überall das Leben aufschliesst. [2, 377]

44, n. 9. Es ist Ein Verhängniss aller Dinge, Ein Leben, Ein Tod; . . . es ist nur eine Welt. [4, 314].

45, n. 4. Dieselbe alles enthaltende und vorsehende Einheit, welche die Bewegungen der allgemeinen Natur, die stillen und stetigen wie die gewaltsamen und plötzlichen Veränderungen nach der Idee des Ganzen mässigt, und alles stets in den ewigen Kreis zurückführt. [2, 374]

In dem Werden und Vergehen der Dinge schaut das All sein eignes heiliges und unendliches Leben an. [7, 168]

Alles also, sofern es in Gott ist, ist selbst absolut, ausser aller Zeit, und hat ein ewiges Leben. [4, 250]

49, n. 4. . . . ein todtes, selbstloses Objekt. [1, 358]

Solange ich selbst mit der Natur identisch bin, verstehe ich was eine lebendige Natur ist so gut, als ich mein eigenes Leben verstehe; . . . sobald ich aber mich und mit mir alles Ideale von der Natur trenne, bleibt mir nichts übrig als ein todtes Objekt und ich höre auf, zu begreifen, wie ein Leben ausser mir möglich sey. [2, 47–8]

50, n. 1. Es gehört dazu der Zug innerer Liebe und Verwandtschaft deines eignen Geistes mit dem Lebendigen der Natur, die stille, nach der Tiefe dringende Gelassenheit des Geistes, damit das bloss sinnliche Anschauen zu einem sinnigen werde. [7, 62]

Den Ausbruch grosser Erdbeben hat, mit veränderter Farbe des Himmels, Traurigkeit und selbst das Wehklagen mancher Thiere verkündet, als ob dieselbe Ursache, welche Berge verschüttet und Inseln aus dem Meere emporhebt, auch die athmende Brust der Thiere höbe. —Erfahrungen, die man nicht erklären kann, ohne eine allgemeine Continuität aller Naturursachen und ein gemeinschaftliches Medium anzunehmen, durch welches allein alle Kräfte der Natur auf das sensible Wesen wirken. Da nun dieses Princip die Continuität der anorganischen und der organischen Welt unterhält und die ganze Natur zu einem allgemeinen Organismus verknüpft . . . [2, 569]

51, n. 4. . . . das Wunder der wesentlichen Liebe (welche allein durch den Gegensatz zur Einheit mit sich selbst dringt). [7, 59]

54, n. 2. In der Natur strebt alles continuirlich vorwärts; dass diess so ist, davon müssen wir den Grund in einem Princip suchen, das, eine unerschöpfliche Quelle positiver Kraft, die Bewegung immer von neuem anfaht und ununterbrochen unterhält. Dieses positive Princip ist die erste Kraft der Natur. Aber eine unsichtbare Gewalt führt alle Erscheinungen in der Welt in den ewigen Kreislauf zurück. Dass diess so ist, davon müssen wir den letzten Grund in einer negativen Kraft suchen, die, indem sie die Wirkungen des positiven Princips continuirlich beschränkt, die allgemeine Bewegung in ihre Quelle zurückleitet. Dieses negative Princip ist die zweite Kraft der Natur. [2, 381]

54, n. 4. Die ewige Natur ist eben der in das Objektive geborne Geist, das in die Form eingeführte Wesen Gottes. [2, 66]

56, n. 2. Vom Moosgeflechte an, an dem kaum noch die Spur der Organisation sichtbar ist, bis zur veredelten Gestalt, die die Fesseln der Materie abgestreift zu haben scheint, herrscht ein und derselbe Trieb, der nach einem und demselben Ideal von Zweckmässigkeit zu arbeiten, ins Unendliche fort ein und dasselbe Urbild . . . auszudrücken bestrebt ist. [*1*, 387]

Dieses Eine in Allem ist erkennbar in jedem Theil der Materie, alles lebt nur in ihm. Aber ebenso unmittelbar gegenwärtig und in jedem Theil erkennbar ist das All in Einem, wie es überall das Leben aufschliesst. [2, 377]

57, n. 5. Da der Grund aller Thätigkeit in der Natur Einer ist, der allgegenwärtig, durch keinen andern bedingt und in Bezug auf jedes Ding absolut ist, so können sich die verschiedenen Thätigkeiten voneinander bloss der Form nach unterscheiden, keine dieser Formen aber kann wieder aus einer andern begriffen werden, da jede in ihrer Art dasselbe was die andere ist. [5, 320]

58, n. 7. Die Natur ist nicht bloss Produkt einer unbegreiflichen Schöpfung, sondern diese Schöpfung selbst; nicht nur die Erscheinung oder Offenbarung des Ewigen, vielmehr zugleich eben dieses Ewige selbst. [2, 378]

59, n. 8. . . . der innere Typus aller Dinge wegen der gemeinschaftlichen Abkunft Einer seyn muss. [5, 325]

59, n. 1. . . . die Erkenntniss der ersten Einheit, aus der alles in der Natur hervorgeht, und in die alles zurückkehrt. [5, 327]

. . . alle aus einem gemeinschaftlichen Grunde fliessen. [5, 320]

Dieses dem Begriff nach ewige in-einander-Scheinen des Wesens und der Form ist das Reich der Natur, oder der ewigen Geburt Gottes in den Dingen und der gleich ewigen Wiederaufnahme dieser Dinge in Gott. [7, 59]

61, n. 8. Jeder der im All begriffenen Einheiten ist also wieder der Abdruck des ganzen All. [5, 378]

CHAPTER 5

62, n. 1. Sie hat eine gefährliche Tendenz ins Statische, und es ist aus ihr für Schellings Indentitätsystem viel Problematik gekommen. Aber dieses Statische ist nur die Kehrseite des von Schelling eigentlich Gewollten. [Fuhrmans, p. 57]

63, n. 2. Nichts ist dem Seyn an sich nach entstanden. [4, 119]

Es lebt ein unveränderliches, sich immer gleiches Seyn. Alle Thätigkeit und Bewegung ist nur eine Betrachtungsweise des Einzelnen. [4, 314]

Es ist nur Geistesträgheit, wenn du die Zeit nicht als die Ewigkeit und die Ewigkeit nicht als die Zeit zu sehen dir bewusst bist. [7, 63]

63, n. 3. . . . ist alles, was geschehen ist, so wie was

geschieht, Produktion, der Einen Intelligenz, welche nicht angefangen hat noch aufhören wird zu seyn. [*3*, 487]

Jeder besondere Moment der Zeit ist Offenbarung einer besonderen Seite Gottes, in deren jeder er absolut ist. [*5*, 288]

Alles also, sofern es in Gott ist, ist selbst absolut, ausser aller Zeit, und hat ein ewiges Leben. [*4*, 250]

64, n. 5. Was wahr ist, ist wie das, was an sich selbst recht und schön ist, seiner Natur nach ewig, und hat mitten in der Zeit kein Verhältniss zu der Zeit. [*5*, 224]

66, n. 9. Uns allen nämlich wohnt ein geheimes, wunderbares Vermögen bei, uns aus dem Wechsel der Zeit in unser Innerstes, von allem, was von aussenher hinzukam, entkleidetes Selbst zurückzuziehen, und da unter der Form der Unwandelbarkeit das Ewige in uns anzuschauen. . . . Sie unterscheidet sich von jeder sinnlichen Anschauung dadurch, dass sie nur durch Freiheit hervorgebracht und jedem andern fremd und unbekannt ist, dessen Freiheit, von der eindringenden Macht der Objekte überwältigt, kaum zur Hervorbringung des Bewusstseyns hinreicht. [*1*, 318]

Die Intelligenz strebt zwar in jedem Moment die absolute Synthesis darzustellen. [*3*, 487]

68, n. 4. . . . im empirischen Bewusstseyn jenes Ganze nur durch allmähliche Synthesis der Theile, also nur durch successive Vorstellungen erzeugt werden kann. [*3*, 482]

71, n. 7. Das Leben aber besteht in einem Kreislauf, in einer Aufeinanderfolge von Processen, die continuirlich in sich selbst zurückkehren. [*2*, 549]

Der Grundcharakter des Lebens insbesondere wird darin bestehen, dass es eine in sich selbst zurückkehrende, fixirte und durch ein inneres Princip unterhaltene Aufeinanderfolge ist. [*3*, 496]

Die Organisation überhaupt ist die in ihrem Lauf gehemmte und gleichsam erstarrte Succession. [*3*, 493]

Die in sich selbst zurückkehrende, in Ruhe dargestellte, Succession ist eben die Organisation. Der Begriff der Organisation schliesst nicht allen Begriff der Succession aus. Die Organisation ist nur die in Grenzen eingeschlossene und als fixirt vorgestellte Succession. Der Ausdruck der organischen Gestalt ist Ruhe, obgleich dieses beständige Reproducirtwerden der ruhenden Gestalt nur durch einen continuirlichen inneren Wechsel möglich ist. [*3*, 491]

So ist in der Aussenwelt ein beständiger Wechsel von Veränderungen, welche sich aber nicht ins Unendliche verlieren, sondern eingeschränkt sind auf einen bestimmten Kreis, in welchen sie beständig zurückkehren. Dieser Wechsel von Veränderungen ist also endlich und unendlich zugleich, endlich, weil er eine gewisse Grenze nie überschreitet, unendlich, weil er beständig in sich selbst zurückkehrt. Die Kreislinie ist die ursprüngliche Synthesis der Endlichkeit und der Unendlichkeit, in welche auch die gerade Linie sich auflösen muss. Die Succession geschieht nur scheinbar in gerader Linie, und fliesst beständig in sich selbst zurück. [*3*, 490]

77, n. 6.   . . . und im Vergänglichen selbst die Blume der Ewigkeit entfaltet. [*2*, 377]

Auf diese Weise schläft wie in einem unendlich fruchtbaren Keim das Universum mit dem Ueberfluss seiner Gestalten, dem Reichtum des Lebens und der Fülle seiner, der Zeit nach endlosen, hier aber schlechthin gegenwärtigen, Entwicklungen, in jener ewigen Einheit, Vergangenheit und Zukunft, beide endlos für das Endliche, hier beisammen, ungetrennt, unter einer gemeinschaftlichen Hülle. [*4*, 258–9]

Eine Pflanze, von der alles, was ist, nur Blätter, Blüthen

und Früchte, jedes verschieden, nicht dem Wesen, sondern der Stufe nach. [*4*, 314]

78, n. 9. Jene Successionsreihe ist nur Entwicklung einer absoluten Synthesis, mit der schon alles gesetzt ist, was geschieht oder geschehen wird. [*3*, 484]

Die Successionsreihe ist, wie wir wissen, nichts anderes als die Evolution der ursprünglichen und absoluten Synthesis. [*3*, 485]

79, n. 1. . . . entsteht in uns die Idee von einer Zweckmässigkeit des Ganzen, die Natur wird eine Kreislinie, die in sich selbst zurückläuft, ein in sich selbst beschlossenes System ist. Die Reihe von Ursachen und Wirkungen hört völlig auf und es entsteht eine wechselseitige Verknüpfung von Mittel und Zweck. [2, 54]

80, n. 3. Diese drei Ideen drücken dieselbe Identität . . . aus. Auch das Schicksal ist Vorsehung, aber im Realen erkannt, wie die Vorsehung auch Schicksal ist, aber im Idealen angeschaut. Die ewige Nothwendigkeit offenbart sich, in der Zeit der Identität mit ihr, als Natur. [5, 290]

92, n. 4. Wer daher den Ausdruck fände für eine Thätigkeit, die so ruhig wie die tiefste Ruhe, für eine Ruhe, die so thätig wie die höchste Thätigkeit, würde sich einigermassen in Begriffen der Natur des Vollkommensten annähern. [*4*, 305]

CHAPTER 6

101, n. 5. Was ist denn nun jenes wunderbare Vermögen, durch welches nach der Behauptung des Philosophen in der produktiven Anschauung ein unendlicher Gegensatz sich aufhebt? Wir haben diesen Mechanismus bisher nicht vollständig begreiflich machen können, weil es nur das

Kunstvermögen ist, was ihn ganz enthüllen kann. Jenes produktive Vermögen ist dasselbe, durch welches auch der Kunst das Unmögliche gelingt, nämlich einen unendlichen Gegensatz in einem endlichen Produkt aufzuheben. Es ist das Dichtungsvermögen, was in der ersten Potenz die ursprüngliche Anschauung ist, und umgekehrt, es ist nur die in der höchsten Potenz sich wiederholende produktive Anschauung, was wir Dichtungsvermögen nennen. Es ist ein und dasselbe, was in beiden thätig ist, das Einzige, wodurch wir fähig sind auch das Widersprechende zu denken und zusammenzufassen,—die Einbildungskraft. [*3*, 626]

102, n. 9. Es erhellt aber eben daraus von selbst, dass es eine höchst unnütze Frage wäre, welchem von den beiden Bestandtheilen der Vorzug vor dem andern zukomme, da in der That jeder derselben ohne den andern keinen Werth hat, und nur beide zusammen das Höchste hervorbringen. [*3*, 618]

103, n. 1. Weder ist das Ideale als solches Ursache einer Bestimmung im Realen, noch dieses Ursache einer Bestimmung im Idealen; keines auch hat einen Werth vor dem andern, noch ist das eine aus dem andern begreiflich, da keinem die Würde eines Princips zukommt, sondern beide, Erkennen wie Seyn, sind nur verschiedene Reflexe aus einem und demselben Absoluten. [*4*, 304]

106, n. 2. Die Natur fängt bewusstlos an und endet bewusst. [*3*, 613]

107, n. 4. Solange ich selbst mit der Natur identisch bin, verstehe ich was eine lebendige Natur ist so gut, als ich mein eigenes Leben verstehe; begreife, wie dieses allgemeine Leben der Natur in den mannichfaltigsten Formen, in stufenmässigen Entwicklungen, in allmählichen Annäherungen zur Freiheit sich offenbaret. [*2*, 47–8]

Nur der Verstand ordnet unter, in der Vernunft und in der Einbildungskraft ist alles frei und bewegt sich in dem gleichen Aether, ohne sich zu drängen und zu reiben. Denn jedes für sich ist wieder das Ganze. [5, 393]

107, n. 5. . . . in die Vernunft, wo sie, ruhend über ihren vergänglichen Werken, sich selbst als sich selbst erkennt und deutet. [2, 378]

Der Mensch, das Vernunftwesen überhaupt, ist hingestellt, eine Ergänzung der Welterscheinung zu seyn: aus ihm, aus seiner Thätigkeit soll sich entwickeln, was zur Totalität der Offenbarung Gottes fehlt, da die Natur zwar das ganze göttliche Wesen, aber nur im Realen, empfängt; das Vernunftwesen soll das Bild derselben göttlichen Natur, wie sie an sich selbst ist, demnach im Idealen ausdrücken. [5, 218]

107, n. 7. Es sind also auch Produkte einer und derselben Thätigkeit, was uns jenseits des Bewusstseyns als wirkliche, diesseits des Bewusstseyns als idealistische, oder als Kunstwelt erscheint. [3, 626]

108, n. 2. Die ewige Nothwendigkeit offenbart sich, in der Zeit der Identität mit ihr, als Natur. [5, 290]

108, n. 4. Denn auch das, was im Einzelnen unrein und verworren erscheint, dient doch in dem ewigen Wesen angeschaut zur Herrlichkeit und Göttlichkeit des Ganzen. [4, 252]

109, n. 8. . . . jene Macht, welche durch unser freies Handeln ohne unser Wissen, und selbst wider unsern Willen, nicht vorgestellte Zwecke realisirt. [3, 616]

110, n. 9. Das Wesen des Ichs ist Freiheit. [1, 179]
. . . so ist das Ich die einige Substanz. [1, 192]

Leben ist die Autonomie in der Erscheinung, ist das Schema der Freiheit, insofern sie in der Natur sich offenbart. [1, 249]

111, n. 5. Diese Thätigkeit ist die Willkür, oder die mit Bewusstseyn freie Thätigkeit. [*3*, 633]

112, n. 7. Der Mensch allein steht auf dem Scheidepunkt des Guten und Bösen; in ihm allein ist das Band beider Prinzipien kein notwendiges. Und so gehört die Fähigkeit zum Bösen gerade zu seiner Vollkommenheit. . . . Das Böse ist nicht naturhaft, nicht tierisch, nicht untermenschlich, sondern spezifisch menschlich und persönlich. [Hartmann, *1*, 170]

113, n. 2. Es ist nämlich keineswegs ihre Wissenschaft, sondern bloss ihre Schuld, dass ein solches Endliches für sie dennoch existirt, und es lässt sich diess nur ableiten aus ihrem von der Einheit abgewandten und eignen Willen, der ein Seyn für sich will, und eben darum weder sich selbst noch die Dinge sieht, wie sie wahrhaft in Gott sind; und da ferner der religiöse Standpunkt eben der des Sehens aller Dinge in Gott ist, ohne Beweis oder weitere Begründung, sondern eben schlechthin und mit gänzlichem Nichtwissen des Gegentheils, so kann auch von diesem Standpunkt aus ein solches Daseyn einer solchen endlichen Welt, als wir beschrieben haben, nur auf die gedachte Weise abgeleitet werden, nämlich durch ein Abwenden des individuellen Willens von Gott als der Einheit und Seligkeit aller Dinge—durch einen wahren Platonischen Sündenfall, in dem sich der Mensch befindet, welcher die als todt, als absolut mannichfaltig und getrennt gedachte Welt dennoch für wahr und wirklich hält. . . . Wir haben gezeigt, dass das Faktum des Daseyns einer solchen Welt im Bewusstseyn der Menschen gerade so allgemein ist als das Faktum der Sünde, ja dass es eben dieses Faktum der Sünde selbst ist. [7, 81–2]

114, n. 6. . . . bringt dieser Mangel jene Stumpfheit und Leblosigkeit des ganzen Gemüths und Geistes hervor, welche das Erbtheil der social-verdorbenen Menschen ist, und, wo zugleich das sittliche Gefühl kränkelt. [7, 19]

118, n. 8. . . . Identität des Bewussten und Bewusstlosen im Ich und Bewusstseyn dieser Indentität. [3, 612]

Freiheit soll Nothwendigkeit, Nothwendigkeit Freiheit seyn. Nun ist aber Nothwendigkeit im Gegensatz gegen Freiheit nichts anderes als das Bewusstlose. Was bewusstlos in mir ist, ist unwillkürlich; was mit Bewusstseyn, ist durch mein Wollen in mir. In der Freiheit soll wieder Nothwendigkeit seyn, heisst also ebenso viel als: durch die Freiheit selbst, und indem ich frei zu handeln glaube, soll bewusstlos, d.h. ohne mein Zuthun, entstehen, was ich nicht beabsichtigte; oder anders ausgedrückt: der bewussten, also jener freibestimmenden Thätigkeit, die wir früher abgeleitet haben, soll eine bewusstlose entgegenstehen, durch welche der uneingeschränktesten Aeusserung der Freiheit unerachtet etwas ganz unwillkürlich, und vielleicht selbst wider den Willen des Handelnden, entsteht, was er selbst durch sein Wollen nie hätte realisiren können. [3, 594]

118, n. 1. Das Bewusstseyn darüber hebt die Unschuld auf und fordert daher auch unmittelbar die Versöhnung und die freiwillige Unterwerfung, in der die Freiheit als besiegt und siegend zugleich aus dem Kampf hervorgeht. Diese bewusste Versöhnung, die an die Stelle der bewusstlosen Identität mit der Natur und an die der Entzweiung mit dem Schicksal tritt und auf einer höhern Stufe die Einheit wiederherstellt, ist in der Idee der Vorsehung ausgedrückt. [5, 290]

119, n. 4. Nur durch jene ursprüngliche Identität des Theoretischen und Praktischen in uns werden die Affektionen in uns zu Gedanken, die Gedanken zu Affektionen, das Reale ideal, das Ideale real. [1, 413]

120, n. 5. Es ist keine Losreissung der Tat, sondern nur eine Abtrennung dem Denken nach: *dies* produziert durch falsche Imagination . . . abgesonderte Existenzen. [Fuhrmans, p. 72]

120, n. 7. Die Wiedergeburt wird damit beginnen müssen, dass zunächst die Göttlichkeit der Natur wieder begriffen wird und die grosse Einheit alles Seins. [Fuhrmans, p. 40]

121, n. 1. . . . den Vogel, der von Musik berauscht in seelenvollen Tönen sich selbst übertrifft, das kleine kunstbegabte Geschöpf, das ohne Uebung und Unterricht leichte Werke der Architektur vollbringt. [7, 300]

Diess sind die unveränderlichen und für alles Wissen feststehenden Momente in der Geschichte des Selbstbewusstseyns, welche in der Erfahrung durch eine continuirliche Stufenfolge bezeichnet sind, die vom einfachen Stoff an bis zur Organisation (durch welche die bewusstlos produktive Natur in sich selbst zurückkehrt) und von da durch Vernunft und Willkür bis zur höchsten Vereinigung von Freiheit und Nothwendigkeit in der Kunst (durch welche die mit Bewusstseyn produktive Natur sich in sich schliesst und vollendet) aufgezeigt und fortgeführt werden kann. [*3*, 634]

Es ist Eine ununterbrochene Reihe, die vom Einfachsten in der Natur an bis zum Höchsten und Zusammengesetztesten, dem Kunstwerk, herauf geht. [*4*, 89]

Nach meiner ganzen Ansicht der Kunst ist sie selbst ein Ausfluss des Absoluten. [*5*, 372]

123, n. 5. Wie die Sonne frei im Firmament steht, alles bindend und einigend in des klaren Lichtes Kraft, so steht das Gemüth der ewigen Natur in der Verkettung selbst als die Einheit und gleichsam als die göttliche Einbildungskraft derselben, frei und unverbunden, als der Quellpunkt alles empfindlichen Daseyns, welcher auch in der sichtbaren Natur als das Herz schlägt, und alles bewegend und umtreibend in ihrem heiligen Leib, jede Regung verursacht und die Innigkeit aller Erzeugnisse. [7, 202]

124, n. 9. Kunst beruht daher auf der Identität der bewussten und der bewusstlosen Thätigkeit. [5, 384; 3, 626 is reproduced above, 101, n. 5]

124, n. 2. Sie ist eine Kunst, ein ästhetisches Durchschauen des geistigen Organismus in seinen Prinzipien, sie reproduziert mit Bewusstsein und Freiheit, was die unbewusste Intelligenz ursprünglich mit Notwendigkeit produziert hat. [Hartmann, p. 142]

125, n. 5. Es ist gleichsam, als ob in den seltenen Menschen, welche vor andern Künstler sind im höchsten Sinne des Worts, jenes unveränderlich Identische, auf welches alles Daseyn aufgetragen ist, seine Hülle, mit der es sich in andern umgibt, abgelegt habe, und so wie es unmittelbar von den Dingen afficirt wird, ebenso auch unmittelbar auf alles zurückwirke. [3, 616]

Diejenigen Regeln, die das Genie abwerfen kann, sind solche, welche ein bloss mechanischer Verstand vorschreibt; das Genie ist autonomisch, nur der fremden Gesetzgebung entzieht es sich, nicht der eignen, denn es ist nur Genie, sofern es die höchste Gesetzmässigkeit ist; aber eben diese absolute Gesetzgebung erkennt die Philosophie in ihm, welche nicht allein selbst autonomisch ist, sondern auch zum Prinzip aller Autonomie vordringt. Zu jeder Zeit hat man daher gesehen, dass die wahren Künstler still, einfach, gross und nothwendig sind in ihrer Art, wie die Natur. [5, 349]

126, n. 6. Der begeisterte Naturforscher lernt durch sie die wahren Urbilder der Formen, die er in der Natur nur verworren ausgedrückt findet, in den Werken der Kunst

und die Art, wie die sinnlichen Dinge aus jenen hervorge-
hen, durch diese selbst sinnbildlich erkennen. [5, 351–2; 3,
626 is reproduced above, 101, n. 5]

130, n. 5. Der Verstand ist eben auch die Vernunft und
nichts anderes; nur die Vernunft in ihrer Nichttotalität,
und er ist ebenso nothwendig und ewig bei der Vernunft,
als das Zeitliche überhaupt bei dem Ewigen ist und es
begleitet. Der Verstand hat kein Leben für sich, sondern
allein durch die Vernunft. [7, 42]

Im Verhältnis zur Phantasie bestimme ich Einbildungskraft als das, worin die Produktionen der Kunst emp-
fangen und ausgebildet werden, Phantasie, was sie äusser-
lich anschaut, sie aus sich hinauswirft gleichsam, insofern
auch darstellt. [5, 395]

131, n. 7. Die Einbildungskraft . . . ist das Vermögen der
Ideen, oder das, was wir theoretische Vernunft nennen.
Dadurch unterscheidet sich die Schwärmerei von der Vernunft, dass jene zügellose Phantasie, diese Einbildungskraft
in den Schranken der moralischen Postulate ist, jene Chimären, diese Ideen erzeugt. [*1*, 431, Anmerkung 1]

Er möchte das, was in jener Idee als ewig und absolut
eins gesetzt ist, getrennt betrachten, und dem, was nur
Realität hat in der Einheit, auch Realität geben ausser der
Einheit. [7, 151]

132, n. 9. Die blosse Reflexion also ist eine Geisteskrank-
heit des Menschen, noch dazu, wo sie sich in Herrschaft
über den ganzen Menschen setzt, diejenige, welche sein
höheres Daseyn im Keim, sein geistiges Leben, welches nur
aus der Identität hervorgeht, in der Wurzel tödtet. Sie ist
ein Uebel, das den Menschen selbst ins Leben begleitet und
auch für die gemeineren Gegenstände der Betrachtung alle
Anschauung in ihm zerstört. Ihr zertrennendes Geschäft
erstreckt sich aber nicht nur auf die erscheinende Welt;
indem sie von dieser das geistige Princip trennt, erfüllt sie

die intellectuelle Welt mit Chimären, gegen welche, weil sie jenseits aller Vernunft liegen, selbst kein Krieg möglich ist. Sie macht jene Trennung zwischen dem Menschen und der Welt permanent, indem sie die letzte als ein Ding an sich betrachtet, das weder Anschauung noch Einbildungs- kraft, weder Verstand noch Vernunft zu erreichen vermag. [2, 13–14]

132, n. 2. . . . denn alle Heilkraft ist nur in der Natur. Diese allein ist das wahre Gegengift der Abstraktion. [7, 19]

Ist doch die Natur noch der einzige Damm gegen die Willkür des Denkens und die Freiheit der Abstraktion! [7, 36]

Denn in dem Mass, als wir selbst in uns verstummen, redet sie zu uns. [2, 378]

133, n. 4. Reproduced above, 113, n. 2.

134, n. 7. Wenn wir die Dinge nicht auf das Wesen in ihnen ansehen, sondern auf die leere, abgezogene Form, so sagen sie auch unserm Innern nichts; unser eignes Gemüth, unsern eignen Geist müssen wir daransetzen, dass sie uns antworten. [7, 294]

134, n. 9. "Das Gefühl kann niemals trügen, weil da Sein und Bewusstsein dasselbe ist," sagt Schleiermacher. [Kluck- hohn, p. 44]

135, n. 3. Die äussere Welt liegt vor uns aufgeschlagen, um in ihr die Geschichte unseres Geistes wieder zu finden. [1, 383]

137, n. 7. Er ist also nur im Werden, oder vielmehr ist selbst nichts anders als ein ewiges Werden. (Daraus begreift man zum voraus das Fortschreitende, Progressive unseres Wissens, von der todten Materie an bis zur Idee einer lebendigen Natur). [1, 367]

Das System der Natur ist zugleich das System unseres Geistes. [2, 39]

. . . das Ringen des Geistes nach der Anschauung der ursprünglichen Natur. [5, 326]

137, n. 9. Die Vernunft gehört aber eben desswegen weder der realen noch der idealen Welt ausschliesslich an. [5, 379–80]

138, n. 2. Die Intelligenz wird also in einer vollkommenen Anerkennung der im Produkt ausgedrückten Identität, als einer solchen, deren Princip in ihr selbst liegt, d.h. sie wird in einer vollkommenen Selbstanschauung enden. [3, 615]

. . . um einst als Sieger und durch eigenes Verdienst in jenen Zustand zurückzukehren, in welchem er, unwissend über sich selbst, die Kindheit seiner Vernunft verlebte. [2, 13]

139, n. 4. Wie können wir jene scheinbar harte Form geistig gleichsam schmelzen, dass die lautere Kraft der Dinge mit der Kraft unseres Geistes zusammenfliesst, und aus beiden nur Ein Guss wird? [7, 299]

139, n. 6. Die Intelligenz strebt zwar in jedem Moment die absolute Synthesis darzustellen. [3, 487]

141, n. 2. Natur ist nicht begrenzt durch das Aussen, Geist nicht durch das Innen; auch ausser uns waltet derselbe Geist, auch in uns dieselbe Natur. [Hartmann, p. 132]

142, n. 4. . . . die lebendige Copula. [2, 374]

Was wir dir im Gegentheil anmuthen, nämlich das Leben der Materie und eines jeden Theils derselben zu erkennen, muthen wir dir nicht an als etwas, das du im Denken erfassen sollst: vielmehr von eben diesem deinem bildlichen Denken sollst du erlöst werden, und wieder eingehen in die ursprüngliche Einfalt des Seyns und des Sinnes, welcher selbst nur die unmittelbare, gleichsam magische Empfindung des Innern und Positiven und das Band deines eignen Wesens mit demselben ist. Nicht das Leben der Natur selbst, auch nicht dein wahrer ursprünglicher Sinn ist verschlossen; der eigne innere Geistes- und Herzenstod verhüllt und verschliesst dir beide. Das wirkliche Sehen des Lebendigen kann allerdings nicht bemerkt werden in jenem tölpischen oder auch hochmüthigen Wegfahren über die Dinge; es gehört dazu der Zug innerer Liebe und Verwandtschaft deines eignen Geistes mit dem Lebendigen der Natur. [7, 61–2]

142, n. 5. . . . diese lebendige Copula des Bejahenden mit dem Bejahten. [7, 224]

143, n. 7. Ist das Band die lebendige Ineinsbildung des Einen mit dem Vielen, so ist nothwendig mit dem Band zumal auch das aus Einheit und Vielheit Einsgewordne. [7, 60]

143, n. 8. Unter diesem Bild der Liebe Gottes zu sich selbst (der schönsten Vorstellung der Subjekt-Objektivirung) ist dann auch der Ursprung des Universum aus ihm und sein Verhältnis zu diesem . . . dargestellt worden. [6, 63–4]
Dieses ewige Band der Selbstoffenbarung Gottes, dadurch das Unendliche das Endliche, und hinwiederum dieses in jenem aufgelöst ist, ist das Wunder aller Wunder, nämlich das Wunder der wesentlichen Liebe (welche allein durch den Gegensatz zur Einheit mit sich selbst dringt), oder das Wunder der Lebendigkeit und Wirklichkeit Gottes. [7, 59]

146, n. 3. Dieses Ereignis bezeichnet unstreitig einen Wendepunkt in seinem Leben. Mit dem Verlust der ihn so völlig liebenden, völlig verstehenden, in seinen Gedanken lebenden mütterlichen Frau verliert er den eigentlichen

Mittelpunkt seines Daseins. Er äussert damals gelegentlich den Wunsch, überhaupt ganz aus der Öffentlichkeit sich zurückzuziehen. Seine philosophische Produktivität scheint erloschen zu sein—in den restlichen 43 Jahren seines Lebens hat Schelling kein einziges grösseres philosophisches Werk mehr veröffentlicht. [Zeltner, p. 38]

INDEX

Art, 143; as continuance of Creation, 120 f.; as part of nature, 121, 126; transformation in, 122; didactic, 127; prophetic, 128
Artificiality, 113
Augustine, St., *The City of God*, 81
Autonomy, 41 f., 48, 110, 142
Awareness, 125, 138 f.; cosmic self-awareness, 107 ff. *See also* Truth

Baillie, J. B., 18 n.
Bateson, F. W., 135, 136 n.
Beach, J. W., 5
Beaumont, Sir George, 127
Being: identical with life, 38 ff.; identical with God, 63; and thought, 102, 105
Bergson, Henri, 11
Beyond, the, Ch. 2 passim, 26 ff.; objects imbedded in, 22
Böhme, Jakob, 11
Both-And logic, 16, 98 ff., Ch. 7 passim; metaphysical sanctions for, 103
Bradley, A. C., 5
Brinkmann, H., 38 n.
Brooks, Cleanth, 152
Bruno, Giordano, 11

Cassirer, Ernst, 52 n.
Coburn, Kathleen, 3
Coleridge, S. T., 1, 3, 27, 41, 74, 177
Creativity, 126, 142; and art, 120 f.
Custom, tyranny of, 113 ff.
Cyclicity, 73, 77, 171 n.
Cysarz, H., 38 n.

Darbishire, Helen, 27 n.
Death, 46 f.
De Selincourt, Ernest, 7, 68, 82, 127, 148
Development, organic, 75 ff., 135, 143
Dialectic, 103, 142; in Imagination, 99
Dilthey, Wilhelm, 7, 11, 29, 39 n.

Emotion, 133 ff.; feeling intellect, 135, 143
Enthusiasm: preliminary definition of, 15; relation to mysticism, 16; active character of, 22; affirmative character of, 23; religious character, 26; pantheistic flavor, 28; youthfulness of, 145; deficiencies of, 146
Equality and hierarchy, 107

211

Yale Studies in English

This volume is the one hundred and forty-fifth of the Yale Studies in English, founded by Albert Stanburrough Cook in 1898 and edited by him until his death in 1927. Tucker Brooke succeeded him as editor, and served until 1941, when Benjamin C. Nangle succeeded him.

The following volumes are still in print. Orders should be addressed to YALE UNIVERSITY PRESS, New Haven, Connecticut.

114. LYON, JUDSON STANLEY. *The Excursion*. A Study. $4.00.

116. SEYBOLD, ETHEL. Thoreau: The Quest and the Classics. $3.00.

117. KNIGHT, DOUGLAS. Pope and the Heroic Tradition. A Critical Study of His *Iliad*. $3.00.

119. DAVIS, MERRELL R. Melville's *Mardi*. A Chartless Voyage. $4.00.

120. WAITH, EUGENE M. The Pattern of Tragicomedy in Beaumont and Fletcher. $4.00.

122. IRVING, E. B., JR. (editor). The Old English *Exodus*. $5.00.

124. QUIRK, RANDOLPH. The Concessive Relation in Old English Poetry. $4.00.

125. MARTZ, L. L. The Poetry of Meditation. $5.00.

126. HOLDEN, WILLIAM P. Anti-Puritan Satire, 1572–1642. $3.75.

129. BRADLEY, JOHN LEWIS. Ruskin's Letters from Venice, 1851–1852. $5.00.

130. LEYBURN, ELLEN DOUGLASS. Satiric Allegory: Mirror of Man. $3.00.

131. LORD, GEORGE DE FOREST. Homeric Renaissance. The *Odyssey* of George Chapman. $3.00.

132. BOWDEN, EDWIN T. The Themes of Henry James. $3.00.

133. NOON, WILLIAM T. Joyce and Aquinas. $3.75.

134. SCHUTTE, WILLIAM M. Joyce and Shakespeare: A Study in the Meaning of *Ulysses*. $4.00.

135. UNDERWOOD, DALE. Etherege and the Seventeenth-Century Comedy of Manners. $4.00.

136. FRANK, R. W., JR. *Piers Plowman* and the Scheme of Salvation. $4.00.

137. BERGER, H., JR. The Allegorical Temper. Vision and Reality in Book II of Spenser's *Faerie Queene*. $5.00.

138. YOUNG, RICHARD B., FURNISS, W. TODD, MADSEN, WILLIAM G. Three Studies in the Renaissance: Sidney, Jonson, Milton. $6.00.

139. HOWES, ALAN B. Yorick and the Critics. Sterne's Reputation in England, 1760–1868. $4.50.

140. TAYLOR, CHARLES H., JR. The Early Collected Editions of Shelley's Poems. $4.00.

141. BLOOM, HAROLD. Shelley's Mythmaking. $5.00.
142. KERNAN, ALVIN. The Cankered Muse. Satire of the English Renaissance. $5.00.
143. PAULSON, RONALD. Theme and Structure in Swift's *Tale of a Tub*. $4.50.
144. RIDENOUR, GEORGE M. The Style of *Don Juan*. $4.00.
145. HIRSCH, E. D., JR. Wordsworth and Schelling. A Typological Study of Romanticism. $4.00.